REMEMBER WEN?

Poems and Short Stories

Rodney Foster

FOURTH PRINTING 2007

ISBN 0-9638604-4-5

Library of Congress Card Number: 96-092307

REMEMBER WEN ?

Copyright 1990 Rodney Foster

All rights reserved.

All excerpts, dramatic presentation, or any other form of reproduction without written permission from Remember When Publishing is strictly prohibited.

Remember When Publishing
c/o Rodney Foster
19, 7th Street West
Dinsley, Trinidad, W.I.
Tel: 868-640-6040

Cover Design: Carole Mauge-Lewis
Illustration: Carlsbury Gonzalez
Caricature: Fitzroy James
Layout Design: Laronda Arnold

Printed and Bound in Trinidad and Tobago by R.P.L. (1991) Ltd.

Remember Wen?

INTRODUCTION
by
MERVYN J O'NEIL

The song writer reminds us "All we are is but feelings". This defines life.

The cleric in requiem reminds us that we live on in the memories we leave behind. The transition between the two extremes, birth and death, results in events and experiences which lend to the accumulation of memories which are left. In this book, REMEMBER WEN?, a collection of poems and short stories, Rodney Foster plays on memories, this fact of human existence. His title, REMEMBER WEN? rouses the nostalgic in us.

The Chinese proverbially state that to know someone, one must know that person's memories.

Foster hopes to have a greater cross-section of people know the Trinidad and Tobago society. In his endeavor to bring knowledge of this society to a greater audience, Foster employs the media of his own memories. He records his experiences as a person born and raised in Trinidad and Tobago and asks us to recall our own memories and experiences as we read his work.

In introducing this work of dedication, realism, and contribution, we must rationalize its need. Remember Wen? helps to place the people of Trinidad and Tobago alongside counterparts of other nationalities, regions and ethnicities who in literature, plays and dramas expose inner virtues and faults.

Remember Wen? embodies ambitions which parallel those of works which play out social experiences in epics.

Foster employs the colloquial language of Trinidad and Tobago in Remember Wen?. His venture into colloquialism is an act which continues the brave tradition of such proponents of dialect as The African American Paul Laurence Dunbar who, before the turn of the twentieth century, cried out the message of his people's cause and virtues on stages around the United States and Europe; and in published works, has left his perception and motivations for posterity.

As a person of Caribbean heritage, Foster's use of dialect continues our break for freedom from negatives of the European influence, for in the enslaved Diaspora and in Colonial Africa, one was deemed cultured and acceptable only when one wrote and spoke "the King's English" consciously and impeccably.

> This is no light matter. For note that even the Caribbean's Nobel Laureate, Derek Walcott, experienced his own dilemma regarding the choice of language. In his poem, A Far Cry From Africa, he agonizes:
>
> Where shall I turn, divided to the vein?
>
> How to choose
>
> Between this Africa and the English tongue I love?
>
> The following excerpt from Dunbar's, "An Antebellum Sermon" expresses the objective and accomplishment of Remember Wen?, while highlighting the tradition of the dialect which it follows:

> We is gathahed hyeah, my brothas,
> In dis howlin' wilderness
> Fu' to speak some words of comfo't
> To each othah in distress.

Remember Wen? is full of companionship and advice. There is symbolism, appeal, and historic recordings intertwined in Foster's "homeboy", humorous writing style. Remember Wen? is an autobiographical collection of short stories and poems with a greater purpose.

Foster captures the human side of growing up in Trinidad and Tobago, and expresses his gratitude for the values bestowed through this experience. He employs a theme of love for the country of his birth, his fellow man, his life, his heritage, and his calling to capture the elements and traditions of the Trinidad and Tobago society which need to be preserved, but alas, are dying.

One cannot help but recognize Foster's point, a commentary on the imperfections of societies and systems, when he mentions the "bad policeman" named Tobias. One cannot help but identify with his experience when he remembers a mentor uncle named "Theo".

As a piece of literature Remember Wen? will find its way into the "body literature" of Trinidad and Tobago alongside other works which hope to capture for posterity endangered elements, and which strive to bring to a larger audience some of the social contents and traditions of Trinidad and Tobago.

Remember Wen? is a valuable work for the following reason among several others. When someone form Barataria writes about growing up in Barataria, and someone from elsewhere reading this writing discovers that there are common elements in our experiences and values, this realization makes a contribution towards the lowering of the boundaries between individuals and communities, a contribution which promotes closer and better societies.

"In this great future, you can't forget your past." — Bob Marley

Dedication

In loving memory of my maternal great-grandmothers, Ma Petite and Margaret Joseph, paternal grandmother, Irene Hollingsworth, maternal grandfather, Joseph Chapman, Ba Joe, stepfather, Ivan George and meh good, good pardnahs: William Douglas Jr., Edwin Murray, Bertie Robinson and Granville Solomon, De Prince.

Acknowledgements

" I can do all things in Christ who strengthens me." Philippians 4:13

This collection of poems and stories is about people, events, places and things and my experiences with them. First, I would like to give thanks to God for being my constant companion on this journey of faith.

Next, I would like to express my sincerest appreciation to all my friends and the characters of my stories. To name them all would take volumes. However, I must take the risk of mentioning a few for their invaluable support : my parents, Herbine Foster and Frances George; my step-father, Ivan George, whose passing was the stimulus for me to take time out and reflect and produce this book; Irene Hollingsworth, my grandmother; my loving wife, Marjorie; my sisters and brother, Monica, Doreen, Paula and Ashley; Carl Jacobs of the Trinidad Guardian and Keith Smith of The Express; Betty Harbison, Gwen Wyatt, Corleon Akka, Mervyn O'Neil, Clarence Harley, Daphne Cuffie, Paul Keens Douglas, Godfrey Chapman, Hermia Justice, Dennis Sankar, Huntley Hoilet, June Patterson, Don and Avril Smith, Delacey Coleman, Mervyn Murrel, Carlsbury Gonzalez, Pamela Ramcheran, Royce Russell, Ako and Fanta Mutota, and Laronda Strayhon. Special thanks to fellow members of the Saturday Morning Literary Workshop, in Los Angeles, The International Black Writers Association and the Rascals.

Finally, thanks to all my brothers and sisters from Trinidad and Tobago, no matter where you call home now. This is the book we all plan to write someday. It contains some of what we repeatedly talk about whenever we meet. I am sure you will discover parts of your lives within its pages. Read on.

Author's Note

"Remember Wen" is a collection of poems and stories that recounts experiences from my boyhood days growing up in beautiful Barataria, and living in Brooklyn and Los Angeles. Most of the topics are what you and I talk about whenever we gather for "ah lime". Next time you and your friends come together, check the number of times you say: "Yuh remember wen?"

"Remember Wen" is a response to the incessant voices in meh head. The reader would note that some pieces are written in Standard English and others are in what is popularly called Trinidad dialect. The voices of the early material were translated to Standard English because back then that was the accepted, "correct" way to put your thoughts on paper. In those days dialect was more oral than written.

Then in the late sixties, up to the present, there was much debate as to the legitimacy of Trinidad dialect as a language, having both an oral and written form. I supported that movement wholeheartedly. I believe that Trinidadians and Tobagonians are bilingual. Therefore, I am delighted in seeing the growing acceptance of the written form of our language. Thanks to the pioneering work of authors and scholars like Paul Keens Douglas, John Mendes, Dr. Lawrence Carrington and many others. After all, is "we ting".

In addition, somebody has to document "Our Story". There have been too many distortions and omissions when we leave it to others to write about us. In that respect, "Remember Wen" is a firsthand description of my journey and some of yours too. "Yuh must know wey yuh come from in order tuh know wey yuh goin. Otherwise yuh might end up in de same place wey yuh come from" is a very popular saying. "Remember Wen" is my contribution to inform the young and remind the not-so-young about "Our Story".

So, my dear friend, sit back, relax and enjoy my first book. You may recognize yourself within its pages.

Yuh gotta know wey yuh come from in order tuh know wey yuh goin. Otherwise yuh might end up in de same place wey yuh come from.

Anonymous

Table of Contents

To My Mothers 1
Daddy 2
People 3
Trinidad 4
It Wasn't Always So 5
Life 8
Self Awareness 10
Limin 12
Meh Cousin Jean 18
Leh Dem Fight 20
School Days 25
De Common Entrance 29
Oil Dong 31
Nicknames 33
Labor Day In Brooklyn 37
De Rumshop 39
A Lovely Day In Brooklyn 43
Hurry Food 45
Wen Christmas Come 47
First Experience 52
Barbers 53
Empathy 55
Good Parenting 57
Yuh Tink It Easy 60
The Last Wicket 62
Celebrities 68
Indian Food 71
Family Gathering 73
The Man 74

Gone But Not Forgotten 77
Desire 79
Sundays 81
Good Friday 84
My Kitchen Table 86
Callousness 87
Ups And Downs 88
Mas In Los Angeles 89
Brooklyn Experience 93
Customs In Puerto Rico 96
Reflections 97
Mausica 99
Brother And Sister 104
The Seasons. 106
Mama I'm Confused 111
My Roots 113
We Own Is We Own 117
Glossary 118

To My Mothers

Frances, who brought me into this world, and Irene,
my paternal grandmother, who raised me.
To them I say,
"Thanks. I love you.
Thanks for the million and one things
you've done for me."
Would to God that I could find the words that adequately
express my love and gratitude;
or that I could perform some deed to show
how dear you are to me, how much I love you.

My Mother
Frances George
Born in Tobago

Great Grandmother
Margaret Joseph
Born in Tobago

Paternal Grandmother
Irene Hollingsworth
Born in Barbados

Daddy

Hi, Dad
Thought I had forgotten you, eh?
Never happen.
There are no mothers without fathers.
Right?
Thanks, Dad, for your significant contribution
 to my being.

Father
Herbine Foster
Born in Barbados

Rodney Foster

People

The universal set contains people.
All are important and play a role.
"Because God don't make no junk."
In set A, are the Talkers;
In set B, the Actors;
In the intersection are the Talkers and the Actors.
In which set are you?

Trinidad

Oh Trinidad, why do I love you so?
Why do I see your virtues, while others see your faults?
Why do I see your beauty, while others only see your ugliness?
I love you for so many reasons; too numerous to list.
However, I'll try.
I love you because you are you, a unique gem in that chain of Caribbean jewels.
I love you because you are the land of my birth, and my roots are deeply embedded in your rich soil and culture.
Twenty-seven years, girl.
That's a long, long time.
No wonder I dream of you daily.
Family, friends and neighbours are dear to me.
They provide me with points of reference.
An appreciation of growth and decline, space and time,
of life and death.
They help me define who I am; where I came from;
and where I'm going or would like to go.
Everybody likes to be somebody.
In Trinidad I am more somebody than anywhere else in the world.
I'm somebody's son, brother, uncle, godfather, ex-teacher, neighbour, cousin, friend, partner, husband and brother-in-law.
Yes, in Trinidad, I know that I am somebody.
Love is very difficult to express in words.
Love should be acted out.
Words seem so inadequate; so imprecise to describe my feelings and yearnings for you, my native land.
Suffice it to say, I love you Trinidad, Trinidad, Trinidad, land of my birth.

It Wasn't Always So

Yuh see meh here in meh three-piece suit an meh
Volvo motorcar, wit degree in dis an degree in dat.
An yuh tink ah have it easy,
An dat ah always had it easy.
Ah tell yuh, looks could be deceivin, oui.
Every true, true Trini from my days would agree.
Well, lemme take dat back.
Only dose who eh shame ah dey humble origins.

Boy, you doh know, nah.
You doh know de price ah had tuh pay tuh "make it".
An de price ah still have tuh pay tuh keep wat ah have.
No Brother, no Sister, my life wasn't no bed ah roses.
My parents had tuh make plenty sacrifice tuh get me where I is today.
So doh take all dese gains fuh granted.
Today, wat is ah right fuh you wasn't always ah right.
Men an women lose dey life so dat you an me could enjoy dem civil rights today.
An de struggle eh over yet.
We have tuh stay forever vigilant because cruel, evil hands ready tuh snatch dem all de time.

Take fuh example, school.
Yuh ever went tuh school witout breakfast or lunch.
"No."
"Well, I have."
Yuh ever beg lodgin by somebody?
"Wat is dat?"

Boy, dat is wen yuh have no place tuh sleep wen de
nite come an yuh fren put you up fuh de nite,
An gi yuh someting tuh eat an ah place tuh rest yuh head till
foreday mornin come.
Most time is on floor a yuh sleep.
Yes, I experience dat.

Yuh mother ever wake yuh early ah mornin an say,
"Yuh have tuh dress early dis mornin. Ah want tuh sen yuh wit
ah message by Mrs. Davis."
Den she gi yuh ah note fuh Mrs. Davis.
On de way, yuh open de note an yuh see some wrong spellin.
But de note clear. Yuh mother want some change "burrow" till
Friday. Or anyting she could afford tuh sen.
Wen yuh give Mrs. Davis de note, she bus out one laugh an yuh
feel shame.
But she wasn't laughin at me; she was laughin wit me.
"Yuh didn't see Marie? Wey you pass tuh come?"
"Third Avenue," ah say.
"Well, Marie must be pass Second Avenue."
An she bus out laughin again.
" Boy, I jus dis minute sen Marie by your mudder wit de same
kinda note."
Both ah we start tuh laugh now.
Yes, accordin tuh Chalkie, yuh gotta be able tuh laugh tuh live
in Trinidad and Tobago.
Den Mrs. Davis gimme ah hand ah green fig wrap up in some
gazette paper.
Dat is we experience.
Wat? Current gorn an yuh cyar watch TV?
Gi T&TEC ah chance.
In my days we didn't have no TV, nah.
Yuh see dat lady ironin in David Moore picture?
 Dat coulda be yuh Grandmother.

An dem coal-pot iron.
We use tuh borrow dem from ah cousin on Eleven Street. Ah use tuh go fuh dem in de mornin before ah went tuh school an return dem well-greased in de evening.

Yuh see booklist.
Wat de teacher want, an wat meh parents could afford was two different ting.
Dey use tuh try hard an get de Readin Book an de Rithmetic Book.
Crayons and drawin book was ah big joke.
Dey say dey wasn't sendin me tuh school tuh become no artist.
Even in high school was tough.
Ah remember once me an George decide tuh tief two Hall and Stevens Algebra book an exchange.
George was goin Emmanuel and I was goin Osmond.
Dem book was expensive, so we decide tuh tief like Robin Hood: tief from de rich an keep because we was poor.
We figure if it was okay fuh Robin, God wouldn't punish we.

Private lessons?
Dat was fuh de shopkeeper an bizness people chirren.
No wonder why dey use tuh come high in test.
Poor people chirren who make it have tuh thank God an dey parents.
So son, daughter, nephew, niece stay in school an learn well.
Knowledge an action is power.
Knowledge witout action is de same as ignorance.

Life

"Life is a series of responses in an ever-changing environment." About four years ago, I heard that statement on a radio station in Los Angeles. I was stuck in the morning rush-hour traffic on the Santa Monica Freeway. Since that day I have frequently pondered over that thought-provoking line. At times I have struggled with its position. Didn't somebody say that "Life is what you make it." Are we in control of the environment that elicits our responses?

Recently an event occurred in my family that reaffirmed my opening statement. Our home environment was permanently changed. My stepfather, Ivan George, died suddenly. Death has an immediacy and power that defies definition.

As I sit and recall the countless responses that one death caused, I can't help but agree that "life is a series of responses in an ever-changing environment". People from all over changed their personal agendas. They had to remake their lives. Not one soul had planned for a death on that day. But life had to go on. Therefore, appropriate steps were taken to deal with that new change in our physical and mental world.

One of the most lasting memories of that humbling experience was the roles played by people: family, friends, neighbors and even strangers. Death can be a unifying force. There was a warm feeling of togetherness that surpassed that of a wedding or the birth of an infant.

I believe that it is man's nature to be good. Given the right environment, all people will respond with goodness and love. Man's problem is how to create a world that promotes these positive qualities.

During my recent stay in Trinidad, I was delighted to see the number of positive changes occurring in the country. Trinidadians and Tobagonians are a resilient people. Not even VAT (Value Added Tax) will dampen their spirit to aspire and achieve. Some of the reports and rumors emerging from the country would make you believe that Trinidad and Tobago is doomed. Far from it. Even these times will pass.

The good still outnumber the bad by a wide margin. However, the media, both local and foreign, have somehow decided that newscasts have to be dominated by negative information and misinformation. Not enough attention or recognition is given to those who are doing good works. Can you imagine what would happen if the media would refocus their lenses on the positive? They have the power to create a better world. However, my friends, we all have a responsibility in creating the environment we desire. The critical question is whether we are willing to make our contributions. As Spike Lee says in his recent movie, we must "*DO THE RIGHT THING.*"

Self Awareness

Where did I develop that self-hate?
That burning desire to be white?
Eureka! Eureka!
In my education, both formal and informal.
Check it out Brother, Sister.
In the home, straight hair was good hair;
Ponds and white powder for a fair complexion.
Who were the heroes in my Readers and fairytales,
The twelve-thirty shows at Ritz Cinema;
The children in the picture who Jesus suffered
to come unto Him;
The priests who sermonized on Sunday
And terrorized staff and pupils on Monday;
The overseas visitors in sleek, black cars
For whom we stood in the sweltering heat
To wave our red, white and blue flags
And shout, "Ray! Ray! Ray!"
And then get the balance of the day off?
White folks, man.
Don't you remember?
Did you have a Tony Curtis muff?
Or did you slick your hair?
Weren't your favorite singers Elvis, Pat Boone,
Connie Francis and Doris Day?
Who were the villains, the butlers and maids in stiff,
white uniforms who said, "Yes Massa, No Massa."
Those always in the servile, stereotyped roles?
Why such words as blacksheep, blackmail, blackguard,
black book and black Friday?

Quite recently a black Judas in "Jesus Christ Superstar".
See what I am getting at, Brother?
Do you still condemn me for aspiring to be white?
For not wanting to identify with those negative characters?
I'm just another brilliant product of a well-conceived scheme.
However, thanks for the current black consciousness movement,
a new day is dawning.
Now I see the light.
Now I know my task:
Re-educate myself;
Re-educate my brothers and sisters;
Unlearn false truths taught by the man.
Come Brother and Sister, let's end this rap.
Knowledge without action is the same as ignorance.
We have a common mission.
True the road is strewn with many obstacles,
But have faith.
We have the will. We must find the way.

Limin

Limin is ah national pastime in Trinidad.
It have all kinda lime:
Sweet lime, sour lime, short lime, long lime, impromptu lime, formal lime, occasional lime an regular lime.
You name it; we have it.

All lime is not de same.
Dat is why ah Trini will arsk yuh, "Wat kinda lime it is?'
If is ah beach lime, de women go bring ting tuh eat; de fellas go bring de drinks.
But it have some bol' face Trini who would turn up at de lime wit dey two long hand swingin.
An is dem so who does eat an drink more dan everybody else.
Yes, boy, some ah we eh easy at all.

Sometimes, in ah lime yuh does want tuh know,
"Who go be dey?"
In Trinidad, dat is very important.
Dat info could tell yuh if tuh walk wit yuh first lady, yuh deputy or go scoutin fuh talent.
Some ah de best relationships an marriage is ah result of bouncing up ah ting in ah lime.
Lime sweet too bad.

Yuh limin habits does go through different stages in life.
Fuh most people dat is de case.
Fuh some odders, yuh leave dem by de corner an yuh come back an meet dem still limin by de corner; in de same spot.

Dey holdin de fort, maintainin de tradition.
Dat is dem role.

In elementary school days, ah guess yuh could say dat goin by yuh fren tuh play was ah form ah limin.
But real limin fuh me start in high-school; wen ah coulda stay out late at night; sittin down on de culvert by de corner.
Yuh does learn ah lot ah ting under dem street lights by de corner.
Some nights we use tuh ole talk an give jokes.
Dat use tuh be fun.
Everybody would try tuh tell ah joke.
But usually it would be two fellas competin tuh see who could make de group laugh longer an harder.

Ah lime by de corner use tuh have some standard topics fuh jokes.
Bullboy jokes was always ah winner.
Like de one bout Ghost who get one bull in de Croisee;
run down tuh Jogie Road; dash in by Andrew parlor;
An arsk fuh ah snowball an milk.
Wen Andrew tell him he eh have no ice, Ghost say,
  "Doh mind dat. Gimme it jus so."
Or de fella who get three bull on de train line in Laventille.
Wen he get de first one so he shout out, "Who get dat?"
Wen de second one register on he back he say,
"Ah better get outah here before I get one too."
On de third one he take orf down de train tracks like one ah dem big, black, ugly steam-engine.
Dey say he whistle like ah train at every stop he pass between Laventille an Curepe.
Yes man, ah good bull could make dumb man talk an blind man see.
It would even make people recite de alphabet backwards.
Doh ever pray tuh get ah bull.
In my days, Boots an Sharko was de best pair ah storytellers an comedians.

Dey use tuh give one anodder fatigue in song, rhyme an straight talk.
No topic was sacred or off limits.
Dey would tell yuh bout yuh mudder, yuh fadder, yuh sister; everybody in yuh family.
Toute monde baggai.
As long as yuh in de lime, one day yuh turn go come wen dey go pong yuh tail.
Ah see big man cry an cut out de lime wen dey couldn't stan de jammin.
If yuh bizness not in order, be careful who yuh limin wit.
In Trinidad is "Mout open, 'tory jump out."
So beware.

One ah de worst tings dat could happen tuh yuh is fuh de fellas in ah lime tuh hate yuh head.
If is in yuh own village an yuh walkin in wit yuh gyulfren is en'less heckle.
One fella might say,
"But Harry, you could do better dan dat. Wey yuh get dat coki-eye, knock-knee gyul from?
Like yuh hard up or wat?"
Or dey might tell de girl,
"Miss Lady, ah see yuh walkin out yuh dog."
If yuh droppin yuh girl back home in she village, an yuh pass some fellas limin by de corner
Den five minutes later yuh pass back an yuh eh see ah soul, prepare tuh run fuh yuh life.
Dem fellas hidin in de big canal an de bushes
An is one set ah big stone in yuh tail.
So doh cut no style on de brothers on de block wen yuh go courtin in anodder neighborhood.

Ah Trini would lime any day;
Some does lime every day.

Limers

An den again it have some fuh who life itself is one big lime.
Dey eh care if Monday fall on ah Wednesday.
One ah de best lime is ah after wuk lime on ah Friday.
Especially after payday.
De lime could take place in de staff room, by ah co-worker house, in ah snackette or in de rumshop.
After ah long week is nice tuh kick back an beat some beers.
In my day, accordin tuh Chalkie, "Ah beer is ah Carib."
Ah drink plenty Carib in meh drinkin days.
Some ah de favorite waterin holes had de beers just right; like Baby Bear porridge.
Dass in Barataria, Dockworkers Club, Three For A Dollar near Lord Harris Square an, of course, who could forget Humming Bird on Frederick Street.

Back in de late sixties, if yuh frens an dem didn't see yuh sippin ah Carib by Humming Bird on ah Saturday mornin, dog was better dan you.
Like me an meh pardners from Mausica had shares in Humming Bird.
Every Saturday we use tuh dress tuh impress;
Bus ah lime on de Drag, in front ah Stephens;
Check out de chicks; be on de lookout fuh Tobias an he police squad arrestin limers;
An den retire tuh some serious beer drinkin by De Bird.
Mankind use tuh be punctual, because who late had was tuh buy de whole lime ah rounds.
If de lime goin nice, we use tuh go up by Dockworkers after De Bird close.
Up dey de price was lower an it had a jukebox.
We use tuh play kaiso, sing an dance.
Ah fella sellin fresh black puddin use tuh come around.
Beer, black puddin, hops bread an pepper sauce is de greatest.
Ah fella could have membership in more dan one lime.

For example, yuh could belong tuh ah group in yuh immediate neighborhood; tesses yuh grow up wit from small.
Den on certain nights yuh could travel an meet anodder group at ah regular hangout.
In high school we use tuh meet by Slammer on Seventh Avenue an de Eastern Main Road.
We had ah group call de Rascals.
We use tuh play All Fours in Mr. Rodney an dem kitchen.
Dat was we club-house.
Sometimes we use tuh buy beers, Charlies Wine or Gold Coin Wine.
We didn't have plenty money but we use tuh have ah good time.

Wen ah start tuh teach, once ah week we use tuh meet by Solo an Carol tuh play Five Hundred.
De players was Solo, called De Prince, Peter, Dela an Alex.
While card playin in de drawin room, ah wicked fish broth cookin in de kitchen.
After de game we use tuh go round de Savannah opposite Whitehall.
De loser had tuh buy coconut water fuh de whole lime.
As ah matter ah fact dem was meh regular limin pardners wen ah leave Trinidad in 1973.

Yuh know why some lime does last so long?
Is because in ah lime sometimes dey does bad talk people or pong dem.
If yuh leave too soon yuh go miss all dat gossip.
But more important, if you leave, dey go pong yuh tail.
All yuh bizness expose.
Even in front yuh face dey will pong yuh;
Imagine wen yuh tu'n yuh back.
Yes man, limin in Trinidad an Tobago is de greatest.

Yuh know someting?
See yuh later, oui. Ah goin an lime.

Meh Cousin Jean

Jean was one ah de few people who keep she promise tuh write meh wen she reach up in de States in 1971.
An is she an Hanny ah went an stay by wen ah finally decided tuh go up tuh de States an further meh studies.
Yes, in dem days, furtherin yuh studies was synonymous wit goin far away in ah cold country tuh study: America, England an Canada.
So ah save up meh money an ah jump on de bandwagon, too.

Prior tuh meh departure in July, 1973, ah did spen de Summer of 1970 in Brooklyn by meh Uncle Theo an he wife, Brenda.
Dat vacation was excitin.
Ah went as far as Dallas, Texas tuh look fuh meh girlfriend, Annette.
I was impressed by wat America, the land of opportunity, had tuh offer de ambitious.
An I had plenty ambition.
So it was jus ah matter of time before ah pack meh bag an take orf.
Doh get meh wrong, ah was doin quite well as ah teacher in Trinidad but there was an adventurous side of me dat wanted satisfaction.
A burnin desire tuh explore de unknown; tuh take on ah new challenge.
It was a growth experience wit all its accompanyin costs an benefits.
So wen meh insistant, ambitious Cousin Jean kept on encouragin meh tuh come out an study, ah was ready an grateful.

Leh meh tell yuh ah lil bit bout Jean.
Cousin Jean from Lot 10, Parrylands, in de deep south.
She is ah unselfish, caring, country gyul wit plenty ambition

who always helpin people an encouragin dem tuh climb one rung higher.
She like dem grown-ups from longtime who always want tuh know "How yuh doin in school?"
Yuh remember dat type?
Well Jean is one ah dem.
She climbin an she want you tuh climb too.
Jean is ah organizer, ah participant, ah doer, ah "can do" person.
Proud ah she roots an she country.

Thanks, Cousin Jean, fuh yuh role in meh Brooklyn experience.
Thanks fuh yuh hi-riser in de livin-room at Sixty Clarkson.
Thanks, Brother Hanny, fuh invitin meh tuh share yuh space.
We come ah long way, Bro.
Dem was nice days, boy.
So Cousin Jean, yuh on meh V.I.P. list.
Keep up de good work.
May God continue tuh bless you abundantly.

Leh Dem Fight

"Miss."
"Yes, Trevor."
"Miss, look dey fightin in de class."
"Look boy. Dey have gun?"
"No, Miss."
"Dey have cutlass?"
"No, Miss."
"Dey have knife?"
"No, Miss."
"Well, leh dem fight."

Dat was Angela's solution tuh de problem.
Very simple an tuh de point.
It was during lunch time at Morvant North Gov't.
An it was a response born of frustration.
Some ah dem chirren was real wild, boy.
Licks an detention was like water on duck back.
Was enless horrors.
So as long as dey didn't have no dangerous
weapons dey coulda fight all dey want.

Teachin could be de most rewardin job; as well as de
 most frustratin.
De tings dem chirren does come up wit does make yuh stand in
yuh shoes an wonder.
Ah remember one day in 1970, John Baptiste was givin Dictation.
In his best voice and intonation, he read,
"The government has declared a State of Emergency."
De whole staff had tuh laugh wen he show we wat ah chile

write, "A state of emerge and see".
We laugh den, but who knows, de pupil musta be psychic.
Look how de country change after de Black Power Movement.
Baptiste sen dat gem tuh ah contest in de Evening News, "I SEE".
He win two ticket tuh go either Empire or De Luxe Theatre.

Anodder time ah nearly ded wit laugh wen ah was doin Spellin.
Ah tell de class spell "bronchitis."
Ah girl write down "brown kitest."
As man, boy, ah had tuh take ah break.
Ah dash out meh classroom tuh show ah few ah meh co-workers.
But who ah could bounce up in de corridor but ah supervisor.
She want tuh know why ah runnin outa meh class like ah madman.
Ah tell she dem chirren cyar spell at all.
It had some ah dem who wouldn't even get ah correct letter in ah word.
"Mr. Foster, you are exaggerating. No child could be that dumb."
An den she challenge meh tuh ah bet.
"Awright," ah say.
She choose de word; an I pick de student.
Ah choose hard-head Trevor.
He did just come from one ah de small islands.
She say, "Son, spell coffee."
An she start tuh stretch out she hand an smile.
Ah keep meh cool an look at Trevor.
He start orf, "Coffee. k-a-u-p-h" an he stop.
Den he start tuh perspire an scratch.
De supervisor get red in de face an repeat de word about four times; stressin de last syllable harder an harder.
"Coffee, coffee, coffee, coffee that you drink for breakfast in the morning.
Do you understand, boy? Coffeeeee."
Trevor say, "Yes Miss," an start over.
"K-a-u-p-h-y."
De whole class start tuh laugh.

Miss how-she-name nearly drop ded.
She storm out de class; ring de silence bell;
an call ah staff meetin one time.
She order all de teachers tuh teach phonics an Spellin every day.

In Arithmetic, Watley gimme ah classic.
Ah was teachin Distance, Rate and Time.
Ah say," Class, if a car is travelling at thirty miles an hour, how far will it go in one hour?"
Sounds easy, eh?
Well, yuh lie.
Watley watch meh straight in meh face and answer,
"Sir, from about here tuh de corner."
In disbelief, ah say "Wat?"
An repeat de question slowly.
Watley look like he was tinkin it over in he head an den answer, "Sir, from about here tuh Morvant Junction."
Ah scratch meh head an start over meh lesson.
Yuh tink teachin easy, nah.
Teachin is ah art.
An teachers is one ah de greatest asset ah nation could have.
Even though de government an some people does take we fuh granted.
Once ah teacher; always ah teacher.
So I is ah teacher first an foremost.
So keep de faith meh Brothers an Sisters.
One day one day congotay.

Teachin also prove tuh meh dat school is de ideal laboratory fuh nation-buildin.
School an de home environment.
Because watever yuh put in de young, impressionable minds dat is wat yuh get out.
At Morvant North, despite de hardships, de whole staff was

committed tuh excellence an hard work.
Dey was convinced dat chirren from Coconut Drive could learn too.
In ah couple years we start tuh see positive results.
We start tuh get passes in de Common Entrance an School Leaving Exam.
John Baptiste teach dem tuh play pan an compose calypso;
Linda McKend teach dem tuh dance fuh Arts Festival;
Harrison Joseph coach dem tuh be ah winnin netball team an win march pass in grand style.
In sports we use tuh hold we end.
Yes, wit ah change in attitude an expectation,
Morvant North was ah force tuh reckon wit in all areas.
Ah was glad tuh be ah part ah dat process.
Teachin is de greatest.
God bless teachers.

Playing Three Holes

Schooldays

"Schooldays were very happy days."
So says de Mighty Sparrow in one of his popular calypsoes.
Wen I think about happy schooldays, I recall those I spent at Barataria E.C.
I remember de games we use tuh play in de big savannah.
Cricket was lots of fun.
Playin "Who get ball bowl, an who out man bat" for forty-five minutes before first bell ring was a nice way tuh start my day.
"Goes In" was a free fuh all version of cricket; it was every man fuh heself; although sometimes two or three fellas would form a partnership tuh try an monopolize de batting an bowling.
It seemed like all de boys in de school use tuh take part in dis game.
There was no wicket an sometimes we played wit several balls.
Wen cricket was out of season, we would either spin top or pitch marbles on de same cricket pitch.
Playing three hole was enjoyable too.
Yuh remember wat takin bokie was like?
Yuh ever get yuh nocks swell up?
Rescue an cockfight use tuh be excitin.
An around sports time was enless competition.
Everybody wanted tuh represent de school or dey house.
Was keen rivalry among de houses an schools in de area.
Football was meh most favorite sport.
Dey use tuh call meh "Ball Jumbie".
Ah couldn't see ah ball at all.
Anyting dat ah coulda kick was good enuff: breadfruit, orange, milk tin, ah leather outercase stuff wit ole cloth or ah real football.
Ah remember wen Achoy buy ah new football.
We was in Exhibition class.

Nowadays dey does call it Common Entrance.
Everybody was he fren.

Yes, man in dem days yuh had tuh have ah Chiney fren or two.
Dey used tuh bring tuh school money every day an treat dey frens.
Achoy used tuh leh meh ride he bike.
He was meh real pardner although ah never went home by him.
He father was real dread.

Wat does amaze me is how we ever learn in school.
Ah doh tink dem English people did really intend fuh we tuh learn, nah.
Jus check out de curriculum from dem days yuh go see wey ah talkin bout.
Sparrow was right again wen he sing, "If meh head was bright, ah woulda be ah dam fool."

Wat individual classrooms yuh talkin bout.
De school was laid out like San Juan Market.
Yuh lucky if yuh had ah screen separatin your class from de others.
If yuh listen good, yuh coulda hear everything dat goin on in de school.
So ah guess de first ting yuh had tuh learn in school was how tuh tune out all de odder voices an noises except yuh teacher own.

Yuh know someting.
We was learnin ah foreign language long before any ah we went tuh college or high school.
All true, true Trinidadian or Tobagonian have two distinct language: Trinidadianese/Tobagonese
an English Language, the Queen's English.
English Language is someting else.
Wen yuh really check out Standard English Language an wat we does talk an how we does tink most ah de time,

yuh have tuh admit dat we bi-lingual.
We people real brilliant, oui.

Yuh remember parsing?
Yes, dat was wen yuh had tuh take each word in ah sentence and say wey it come from, wey it goin an all kinda choopidness.
For example, if was ah noun, yuh had tuh give de gender, de number, de person and de case.
Ah tort was only people had mood.
But verb had mood, voice, number and tense.
Is one set ah ting yuh had tuh learn bout dese words tuh qualify as "bright."
Den yuh had tuh take ah exam dat make up in England and even sen it back tuh England fuh correction.
Ah doh believe dat Davidson an Alcock, an Mr. London and Mr. Cambridge did expect we tuh learn dat stuff, nah.
But we did.
We people is the greatest.

Well, doh talk bout Arithmetic.
Dat was like ah foreign language too.
Most ah dem sums an dem didn't make sense at all.
Imagine we use to do problems wit pounds, shillings and pence an none ah we never see ah pound, much less spend one.
De only pound I did know was ah pound ah dis an half-pound ah dat in Mr. Chen shop.
Ah mean who cares wen two men go finish diggin ah ditch if dey start wukkin at six o'clock, an stop half-hour fuh lunch.
De correct answer fuh dat in Trinidad is "It depends."
Yes, it depends on if is DEWD workers yuh talking bout.
Dem eh go finish dat ditch til next election.
Ah didn't like History at all.
His Story was not really Our Story.
Yuh dig it, Bro?

All dem set ah dates and battles was too much fuh me.
After all, Henry Morgan an dem was nutten more than crooks wit de King an Queen's blessings.
Tuh besides ah pirate is ah tief, plain an simple.
Ask de Mighty Shadow.
Perhaps dat is why meh best subjects was recess, lunchtime and dismissal.
However, seriously speakin though, somewhere along de line somebody or someting convince meh dat if ah learn all dem subjects ah would become "somebody in life."
Must be de licks an duncey cap ah did fraid dat make meh learn; or perhaps ah didn't want tuh disappoint meh parents.
Dey had tuh sacrifice tuh sen meh tuh school.
Or was it because ah was tryin tuh impress one ah dem straight hair, high color girls who used tuh come high in test?
Watever de reason, ah glad ah learn enuff so today ah could pick sense outa nonsense.
Ah guess ah have tuh put meh schooldays in context; put dem in de right perspective.
It was de best ting dey had tuh offer den an we did "The Right Thing."
Or did we?

De Common Entrance

Yuh tink it easy tuh sit an above all pass de Common Entrance exam.
One third of thirty-six thousand go pass;
de remainder go be repeatin or scruntin either in a Post Primary class, a mediocre private secondary school, or limin on de block ketchin dey tail.

Boy, dis exam is someting else.
Ah set ah blocking out, plenty directions and tricky questions.
In all seven sections, adding up tuh two hundred and forty questions and lasting about four hours.
Real mental torture fuh we lil kids.
Excuse me, ah mean child prodigies.
Yuh know someting, boy?
No O'Level or A'level exam does last so long.

Monday tuh Saturday is ah set ah drill, based only on C.E. material.
Wat Games and Gardening yuh talkin bout.
Not even ah lil Social Studies and Science.
Dem doh come fuh de exam.
Sir say we go do dem wen we pass.
We class specializin in C.E. products.
Sparrow didn't have no C.E. exam, so he schooldays did bong tuh be happy.

"Chile, wey yuh teacher tink bout de exam?"
"Ma, Sir say de exam is ah criminal exam.
He wonder if dem big boys could pass it.
But he say he cyar do nutten.

He have tuh conform tuh de wicked system
Otherwise is victimization fuh he an he family.
Yuh tink it easy, Ma?
De scene real terrible.
Dem big boys have vested interest in de scheme.
Even Sir makin he lil ting.
Two hundred tax-free dollars ah month in private lessons.
Others sellin books at two dollars plus.
Is ah real lucrative bizness.
Ma, yuh tink dem criminals go kill dat goose?
Never happen in Congotay.
So is Common Entrance evermore fuh we class.
So Lawd, help yuh boy tuh block out correct and pass.

Oil Dong

Aye, hear nah man.
Gimme ah piece ah chicken dat I could identify.
Me eh like dis patty bizness at all.
Patty eh have no bone; an yuh know dat every true, true Trini like he bone.
He like tuh eat de meat, suck de bone an den chew it up fine, fine.
Jus arsk meh sistah, Doreen.

So de odder day wen was lunchtime on one ah dem big airline; an dey serve chicken patty ah was real vex.
Wen I man hungry ah doh make joke wit meh food.
Perhaps de reason ah make ah fuss an long up meh mout was because ah did know dat jus above meh head in de overhead compartment was ah serious oil dong.
Meh lovin mudder did get up early an start she pot.
Trinidad mudders is de greatest.
De breadfruit was straight from Stellene in Barbados;
an de coconut was from Uncle Newton in Tobago.
De pigtail an green pepper was from Tunapuna market.
Man, yuh shouda smell dat pot.
It wake up everybody.

Perhaps dat is why ah nearly tell de smilin air hostess tuh take back she oily patty an rice pilaf, an han meh meh mudder oil dong.
But ah decide tuh act cool an sophisticated.
Yuh see, across de aisle was three Vincentian-lookin fellas, an ah didn't intend tuh share meh food wit no strangers.
Yuh know how dey say breadfruit is Vincentian beef.

Furthermore, meh mudder did done tell meh tuh make sure an gi meh wife, Marjorie, an meh sister, Paula, some ah de oil dong. So American, wen yuh have Trini on board yuh plane, doh serve no patty.
Serve chicken wit bone in it.
Even if is back'n' neck self.

Nicknames

Havin ah nickname in Trinidad an Tobago is traditional.
In fact, not havin ah nickname is like being left out.
Everybody who is somebody in de country have ah nickname.
Whether is complimentary or derogatory is besides de point; an whether you know dat you have ah nickname doh really matter.
Jus de fact dat some people call yuh by anodder name is sufficient tuh qualify yuh fuh membership in "De Nickname Club."

All my fren an dem had nickname.
As ah matter ah fact, some ah dem had more than one.
Some ah dem dey real name was like ah nickname because it was so uncommon an jokey.
Take fuh example, ah fella wit ah name straight from de Old Testament.
Ah mean who in dey sound mind go watch ah nice, lil baby boy an call him Zaccahrias.
Wen he grow up everybody go call he "Zack."
Yuh remember Sparrow singin bout Erasmus B. Black.

Ah nickname could be based on physical features.
So names like Boxhead, Pinhead, Headmaster, Header an Tete all had tuh do wit de shape an size of yuh head.
Ears was anodder popular part of yuh body.
So Bat Ears, Donkey, Batty Ears an Dr. Spock was common.
Big Nose, Rubber Nose, Snatty Nose an de names of characters who was famous fuh dey nose was anodder source of nicknames.
In Barataria we had Cyrano, Karl Malden and Pinocchio.
De shape of yuh mouth could also lan yuh ah lastin nickname.
Fuh example, everybody in Barataria E.C. School could

remember Sapat Mouth an Zip Mouth.
Dem fellas didn't like dem name at all.
But de more yuh didn't like yuh nickname de more it stick.
Ah remember once Zip Mouth gimme bout four hurry calpet.
Ah didn't know he coulda run so fast.

Sometimes ah whole family could have one nickname.
Yuh remember Chicken an dem.
Dem was real skinny people.
An Ducklin an dem from Nine Street.
De mother was small an skinny but she use tuh wuk hard fuh so.
She use tuh wuk from sun-up tuh sundown; mindin cow, washin, totin water an cookin.

In my day, Black Boy wasn't ah nice nickname at all.
Dat use tuh cause plenty fight.
Dat was before James Brown sing,
"Say it loud. I'm Black an I'm proud."
Before dat, you call ah man Blackie Pokey, prepare tuh run or fight.
Whitey Cockroach was de name fuh de baccra.

It was common fuh more dan one person tuh have de same nickname even in de same village.
So names like Tall Boy, Shorty, Fatman, Turkey, Ghost, Shadow, Big Belly Doon-Doon, Big Foot an Thin Foot was quite common.

Some people had some real complimentary names.
Yuh remember "De Doctah or De Doc."
People did real like he, boy.
Although some of his detractors use tuh call him "Deafy".
"Sweet Walks" was ah nice, shapely, brown-skin chick from Eleventh Street.
Wen she walk dong de street in ah tight pants or ah mini skirt, mankind use tuh stop talking an jus stare an salivate.

She was bad fuh days an she know it.
Einstein was ah bright fella who use tuh wear some thick, thick glasses an go college.
Everybody say he woulda be ah doctah or some kinda scientist.
Den it had de poets: Shakespear an Keats, an Socrates an Aristotle de village philosophers.
An, of course, it had de pious-looking fella who was ah arcolyte; we use tuh call him "Priest."
In addition tuh dem names, it use tuh have some real original nicknames too.
Like "Clock," de fella who had ah good right hand an de part dat remain after ah badjohn chop orf piece ah he left hand.
Hop 'n' Drop an Hoppy was two fellas wit uneven legs.
"Beep" was ah fat Indian man in ah kakhi uniform who use tuh sell ice-cream in all de cinemas in San Juan an all over Barataria.
"Somebody Call" was anodder fat Indian man from who yuh coulda "Get yuh pure, ground back pepper" in San Juan Market on Sundays.
He also use tuh appear at all major sportin events sellin de best fry channa ah ever taste.

Ah know yuh cyar wait tuh hear my nickname so I eh go disappoint yuh.
In meh boyhood days, Dalma call meh Jaimey, after ah character in de Phantom comic strip.
Tall, lanky Dalma, "Daddy Long Legs," had a name fuh everybody. Wen he christen yuh so, yuh stuck wit dat name fuh de rest ah yuh life.
Arsk Moses, Zwill, Sharko, Pigmy Aja Tan Tan Bo Hog, an Boobs.
In high school de Rascals use tuh call meh Pizon.
An in Mausica was Dolphus, short fuh Adolphus, meh middle name.
As yuh grow older, nicknames could cause yuh plenty embarrassment.

Yuh ever bounce up ah schoolmate an all yuh could remember is dey nickname?
Or de nickname of de brother or sister?
Ah mean tuh say, how yuh go greet de respectable-lookin citizen in de presence of his wife an chirren wit, "Wey going on Sapat Mouth?"
Or arsk de nice-lookin craft, "You is Puddin sister?"
So sometimes wen yuh see people pass yuh straight in tong an yuh cocksure dey see yuh because you an dem eye make four, doh dig nutten.
Is not because dey eh recognize yuh or dey playin ting wit deyself.
Is simply because dey cyar remember yuh real name
an dey too embarrass tuh admit it.
Aye, by de way, all dis time ah runnin meh mout, tell meh someting, "Wey is your nickname?
Ha! Ha! Ha! O Lawd. Oh name boy."

Labor Day In Brooklyn

Labor Day is the happiest day in the year for me.
Labor Day rejuvenates me and gives me energy to
survive in this concrete jungle.
It's a good substitute for my Trinidad Carnival.

Labor Day to me means many things:
a grand family reunion, a once a year event to renew
and establish relationships, a time to trade information and
gossip, to pass the bottle from mouth to mouth like a
communion cup, and to eat and drink as though there were no
tomorrow.

Labor Day is typically West Indian.
Sincere greetings richly flavored with obscene language
is common, as dear friends meet and embrace;
stand back and check out one another
and exchange numbers, addresses and promises.
Just as they did last year.

So my fellow West Indians.
Native Americans too.
Come join me on September 4th on Eastern Parkway.
Meet Rose, Kitch, Sparrow, Nebulae an Lion an
The Naturals and leh we jam.
Leh we jump and wine to steelband, calypso, reggae,
brass and soca and have a jolly good time.

In De Rumshop

De Rumshop

Yuh know is one ting ah always promisin tuh do every time ah go home.
Dat is tuh go an drink rum in ah rumshop.
No man, not ah snackette like Roy Snackette on Third Avenue.
Not even ah club like Lucky Jordan in town.
Ah mean ah simple, down-to-earth rumshop like Mr. Chen own.
De kind wey does have groceries sellin on one side an liquor on de nex side.
An it have two swingin doors like in dem Western ah use tuh go an see by Ritz theatre.
An it have ah sign in de shape of ah hand wit ah index finger pointin.
De sign say "URINAL."
Ah remember de first time ah had ah hot pee an went in de urinal.
Ah nearly ded.
Wen de strong smell of ammonia hit meh so, de pee went back.
De urinal was ah half ah drum with some camphor balls in it.
It was stink, stink, stink . . .
An tuh make matters worse it was emptyin in ah drain leadin tuh de same canal dat we use tuh run jockey race in.
Wen ah tell meh fren an dem, we stop runnin jockey race in dat canal.
Yes man, yuh have tuh be real drunk tuh use de urinal in de rumshop.
In dem rumshop yuh does have tuh call de shopkeeper from sellin saltfish an flour tuh come an sell yuh ah flask or petit quart ah rum.
An den sell yuh chaser an gi yuh glasses wit ice.
Dat is wat I want tuh do real bad.

It use tuh look like dem big men an dem use tuh be havin ah good timie.
An I love ah good time.
Ah remember how Lenny an S.M. use tuh beat de counter an knock bottle an spoon an sing calypso.
Mr. Lenny use tuh sing "Royal Jail" better dan Sparrow;
an S.M. use tuh chime in wit ah melodious "All Stars."

Mr. Chen rumshop use tuh be integrated;
so yuh coulda hear both Indian tune and kaiso.
Dem men use tuh sound real happy tuh me.
Now an den it would have one or tow women but most ah de time was only men.
Yes, sometimes dey use tuh cuss an fight, but most time it was peaceful.

Aye, hear nah man, I believe Robbie an he government could solve de country problems tomorrow.
Jus hol Parliament meetins in any rumshop in Trinidad and Tobago.
Under de influence ah alcohol dem fellas sure tuh come up wit some good solutions tuh we problems.

Yuh ever really listen tuh dem men arguin in ah rumshop? Is de greatest.
Dey does have answer tuh every topic under de sun.
For example, on de question of de death penalty, one man would shout out:
"I say dey should hang dey so-an-so."
Anodder one would disagree an say:
"I say lock dem up an throw way de key.
Feed dem on bread, water and salt."
Philosophical issues is de greatest.
Is dey man does start tuh use big words an even invent some new ones.

On de question of right an wrong, ah fella in ah ole jacket an tie would stand up; hol he suspenders an, wit spit flying in all direction, start, "Categorically speaking, I always believe ah right ting is ah right ting."
He pardner would interrupt him an arsk,
"Wey is yuh point, Harry? Wey is yuh point?"
Harry would look at him wit scorn an den continue,
"As I was emphatically narrating before I was so rudely interrupted by my obstreperous collegiate here, I always believe . . ."
De whole group would shout, "Look, Harry why yuh doh shut yuh mout an siddong. Yuh talkin choopidness. Here, take anodder drink."
"Aye, Uncle, bring anodder bottle fuh de boys.
Put dat on my bill."

Yes man, rumshop is ah institution in Trinidad an Tobago.
Is ah forum fuh all kinda discussion, an disseminatin an gatherin information.
Some call it gossip, others call it oletalk.
Long ago it was strictly de domain of men.
No respectable woman would be seen in de vicinity of ah rumshop.
Although it had some brave women who didn't care bout no respectability wen it come tuh collectin de rent money or de money tuh buy food fuh de chirren.
Dey use tuh block de man by de door an demand de cash before he drink out all wit de boys.

Nowadays tings change.
Ah pardner tell meh dat ah woman embarrass ah man in front all he frens an he eh do ah ting.
Dis Romeo was givin he common-law wife some horrors wit ah young chick.

So she decide tuh do fuh him.
She come down by de rumshop dress tuh kill.
If yuh see mini.
In ah loud voice, she shout out, "Aye, Harry, yuh know yuh shouldn't be drinkin all dat set ah rum.
Yuh know wey does happen wen nite come.
All yuh does want tuh do is sleep.
Ah cyar take dis frustration no more. Ah gorn."

Ah hear everybody stop drinkin an turn up
dey macometer.
In two-twos Harry disappear.
He eh even pay Mr. Chen fuh he rounds ah drinks.
De talk is dat de Village Ram plantin garden in Toco.
Denise Plummer right, oui.
Nowadays "Woman Is Boss."
So nex time ah come Trinidad, ah headin straight fuh de rumshop.
Meet meh either by Mr. Chen or Dass.

Lovely Day In Brooklyn

Indeed it is a lovely day.
Dear King Sol is out in all his splendor.
And the kids, mostly Blacks and Hispanics and a few Whites
have all come out to play: hand-ball, riding, skipping and
bathing at the specially fitted hydrants from which jets of
sparkling water shoot into the air only to
cascade onto the bodies of the frolicking children and into the
vehicles that pass by.
Shrieks of delight add to the city noises as everyone enjoys the
arrival of Summer.

Lined up against the monstrous buildings are the well-dressed
aged:
Senior citizens, the majority women.
The scene reveals a sociological fact.
"The neighborhood is changing."
Mere euphemism, Brother.
What they really mean is that minority groups: Blacks and
Hispanics are steadily replacing the Whites.
It's called urban flight.
The middle-class whites are fleeing to the suburbs.
Some of the old have retired to "sunny Florida",
leaving behind this patient group who escape the boredom of
their musty apartments and sit in their aluminum chairs
while King Sol caresses their pallid skins.

Their occupations make an interesting study:
some knit, read or are read to by their Black nurses,
others gossip and exchange memories.

A few, canes at their sides, limbs trembling uncontrollably, make small talk with babes in arms and toddlers.
Each one comments on the beauty of the weather.
"Nice day, isn't it? Lovely Weather."
As I absorb these scenes, I begin to question myself.
Is this progress?
Is this civilization?
I feel myself running; running from this concrete jungle, back among "the Forest People".
And I think aloud, " Must the road to Utopia be like this? "

Hurry Food

Aye, yuh remember dem hurry pot yuh mudder use tuh cook longtime?
Dat food sweet too bad.
Ah could still remember one ah de hurriest pot, corn beef an rice.
Every now an den, I mehself does drop ah corn beef an rice on dem.
In two-twos I could fix yuh up.

Man, you gi my mudder some bhaji or dasheen bush, ah dry coconut, some rice, quarter pound ah pigtail an quarter pound ah saltfish an two head ah garlic; an yuh could end up scrapin de pot, eatin de bun bun an beggin fuh more.
Dat lady is de greatest.
She could teach all dem chef in Hilton a ting or two bout basic, everyday, Trinidad cookin.

But de hurriest food was macaroni an egg.
Like wen yuh come home from school ah lunch time
an yuh mudder eh start cookin yet.
Eider because she was ole talkin wit de neighbor an de talk was too sweet;
Or she get caught up in listenin tuh Dr. Paul or Portia Faces Life.
Well, before yuh could say Jack Robinson; she boil up some macaroni quick, quick, quick, scramble two egg;
mix dem up wit some salt butter; an yuh have someting hot tuh put in yuh stomach until later.

By de way, yuh remember sugar-water?
Yes, dat was poor people juice.

Dat was de original health food drink.
No preservative.
Just plain pipe water an Caroni brown sugar.

Not everybody could cook ah good hurry pot.
It take special skill an creativity.
Yuh eider have it or you don't.
Yuh have tuh learn dat by watchin yuh folks
from de time yuh small.
Hurry pot an fast food is two different ting.
Hurry pot have personality, class an good taste.
Arsk any true, true Trini an he go tell yuh wat ah mean.

Wen Christmas Come

"There's no place like home for the holidays." So says a popular Christmas song. Since I am incurably romantic, around this time of year, home for me is Trinidad, 23, Twelfth Street, Barataria, to be exact. It was there that I spent the most enjoyable Christmases to date.

Ah set ah vivid memories does come tuh meh head. Ah does remember de set ah cleanin an decoratin we use tuh do fuh Christmas. Like stainin de floor wit mahogany stain an den polishin it tuh de sound of music. And scrubbin out de kitchen an changin de linoleum.
Ah use tuh enjoy goin in de Croisee an buyin de linoleum. Yuh shoulda see meh takin de back roads on meh bicycle ridin one han, wit de roll ah linoleum under meh left arm like ah lance. Ah was like Ivanhoe in ah joustin contest.

Ah does remember buyin postcards for four cents by Texas Studio, at de junction of Fifth Street and El Socorro Road. Den goin by San Juan Post Office an buyin stamps at ah penny each. In dem days ah was in Exhibition class. Dey call it "Common Entrance" now. We use tuh save up an do chores tuh get enuf money so dat we could sen cards tuh we parents, relatives, teachers an frens.

Christmas time in school use tuh be fun. Test time was excitin. Ah use tuh try meh best tuh battle up wit dem shopkeeper and drugstore owner chirren. Every term meh parents use tuh promise meh ah bike if ah do good in test. If ah did get all dem bike dey promise, ah woulda have more bike dan Sports and Games. Anyhow, de promises motivated meh. Ah get meh first bike in High School.

Last day ah school, "Tiefin Day", use tuh be ah treat after dey call out de test results. Ah tink it was de Rapsey family from Aranguez Estate dat use tuh sponsor dat fete. It was great fun tuh get ah whole Solo fuh yuh own self. Dat an ah bag wit ah cupcake an some sweetie. Every year ah does wonder how Barnes, meh good fren, who I aint see since we leave elementary school, use tuh get so much cake crumbs down in he red Solo. Den he had de nerve tuh arsk people if dey want tuh trade ah sip. He musta be crazy.

Ah remember how we use tuh visit one another homes fuh de holidays. Just tuh eat, drink, maco an play games like "Stick Dem Up" an "Snakes And Ladders". Boobs never get shoot or kill yet. Bullet always missin him or just grazin him. Once ah shoot de man point blank range. He say meh gun didn't have no more bullet because ah did empty it on de two fellas ah shoot last. Boobs shoulda be ah lawyer.

In elementary school days, we use tuh drink plenty sorrel an ginger beer. As we get ah lil older, dey started tuh gi we Carypton, Kola Tonic an Cider. Ah eat enless cake: black cake, marble cake, sponge cake an sweetbread. Dates, nuts, apple, grapes, portugal an sweetie went down de hatch too. Better man belly bust dan good food waste.

As we grow older an de fellas start tuh have gyulfrens, dat was someting else. Christmas time is one time yuh does find out how yuh rankin. De kind ah postcard, an de size an quality ah de gift yuh get does tell yuh dat. In some years it use tuh be ah special item. Ah remember de year like town did say "Banlon Jersey fuh yuh man". Man, Habib's an Manshop make ah jail fuh dem. Ah smile like ah king wen, Heather, meh gyul from Couva, bestowed ah beige Banlon on meh. Yuh tink it easy. Christmas fuh me is hearin certain classics by singers like Nat King Cole, Bing Crosby, Nap Hepburn an ah local singer name Kelwyn Hutcheon. He use tuh sing "Kiss Me For Christmas". Ah mean wat would de season be witout songs like White Christmas, Listen Mama. Jingle Bells an, of course, Drink Ah Rum An Ah Poncha Crema by Kitch.

In addition tuh de traditional songs, some years use tuh have ah special tune. Like one year was Gemini Brass playin "Higher and Higher". Ah nex year was Bryner singin "Rich Man, Poor Man". In dem days, yuh use tuh hear de tunes on de radio or play dem on yuh record player or radiogram. Today everybody have stereo equipment. Who could forget de year wen Ed Watson an Kitch drop "Sugar Bum-Bum" on we. Man, if yuh didn't have dat record in yuh house, dog was better dan you. Dat was fete fadder. An wat about de year dat Crazy "Nani Wine" an Baron "Somebody" had people dancin. Dem tunes mash up de place, boy. Yes man, nowadays Christmas is ah mixture of Soca an carols.

Christmas is parang wit meh pardners from Mausica: Noel T, Beck, Alisford, K.B, Wallace an Harry Joe, an de Rascals: Slammer, Raymond, Gordon, Frank, Carlton, Kenneth, Jeffrey, Cecil, Tony an Livers. We use tuh have ah ball. Christmas is also ah riddum section: ah group ah fellas wit ah tenor pan, ah doo-dup or ah box-base, some guitar an two-three chac-chac an, of course, some iron. We use tuh go from house tuh house beatin people stocks.

Ah will never forget de year wen John Baptiste inform Miss. Janet dat he doh eat diced ham. He want only slice ham. Man, ah feel so shame fuh meh pardner dat ah crawl under de table. Janet run quick, quick an bring out some sliced ham. Yuh shoulda see how everybody get down on both de slice ham and de diced ham. If yuh see dem teachers from Morvant North comin, take orf yuh lights an lock up tight, tight. Dey not easy at all. Dey like dem social moppers dat Sparrow sing bout.

Two memories does always make meh laugh. One was wen three teachers finally catch up wit ah fellow-teacher who stocks nobody ever beat. He was one ah dem who always have ah "prior engagement" or always "just on the way out". Yuh know dat kind? Well, on dis particular day it was pourin rain. Bucket ah drop. Dey call an tell him dat dey was jus ah few houses away an dey comin over. Who tell him say "All Right"?

Dey was in Tunapuna. Ah hear dey speed down de road usin all kinda back road. Wen dey reach San Juan an exchange season's greetins an ting, de fella bring out ah new ball, ah full, unopened bottle ah Ballantine Scotch Whisky. He also bring out ah whole black cake. Man, ah hear dem two guys an de lady went tuh wuk on de stocks wit ah vengeance. One fella get so tight he even take ah shower an resume de attack. I eh callin no name. But if you call name ah go whistle. Later dat evenin wen HJ, S an Miss. J related de story, de whole lime laugh until we cry. Ah tell yuh, look out fuh dem teachers from Morvant. Dey aint easy at all.

De odder hilarious event was wen some fellas tief Mr. an Mrs. X ham. Mrs. X bawl like ah cow wen she discover dat she ham was missin from she pitch-oil pan dat was on three big stone in de backyard. De fellas take de ham jus before de bone shoot, an put ah big stone in de water. Mrs. How-she-name couldn't believe she eyes an she ears wen de fork bounce back. She say it was ah expensive Virginia ham. De kind dat does come wrap in tar-paper. De husband grab he cutlass an start tuh cuss. He threaten tuh kill dey so-and-so. Nobody aint see ah ting because people say de family use tuh get orn too social an stuck-up. Dey tink dey was better dan everybody else. Ah hear dey had was tuh run quick an trust ah ham by Mr. Chen. For weeks we use tuh pass in de night an sing, "Jonah, you tief ah ham here?"

By de way, Christmas is also pork. Yes, Master Willie an Miss Piggy. Ah cyar imagine ah good Christmas witout pork. Ah must have meh ham an ah piece ah roast pork. If yuh have some pig ears souse an some black puddin from Shadow or Charlies, so much de merrier. So all ah alyuh who suddenly discover dat pork eh good fuh yuh, I glad too bad. Is more meat fuh me.

Wit all de excitement goin orn we use tuh remember de significance of de celebration, de birth of Christ. So goin tuh church was ah integral part of de observance. We use tuh go tuh St. Colombo Anglican Church. De church use tuh be pack. De service use tuh be beautiful, wit de choir soundin like angels. Yes man, at Christmas time church was someting else.

Yuh know someting. Dis book eh have enuf page tuh really do justice tuh all my fond memories of Christmas in Trinidad an Tobago. Ah sure some ah my memories is yours too. So as yuh celebrate dis joyful season, remember de good ole days. Spread goodwill an love. Have ah happy Christmas an ah prosperous New Year.

First Experience

So this it, eh?
This is the wondrous snow.
Look how the snowflakes drift lightly by,
settling on the ground below.
Steady is the pile up.
Lord, when will it stop.
Much later. . .
Wow! What a transformation!
The ground now is a plush white carpet.
Autumn's leafless trees are now leafed with
crystal clear icicles.
Branches break under their weight exposing jagged,
yellow-brown scars which stand out against the
dazzling whiteness.
The scene is indescribable.
Through the heavy doors and into the street I go.
Cold and piercing winds to meet .
Feel the soft sprinkle of flakes against my cheeks.
And hear the crunch, crunch beneath my feet.
See the children frolic to and fro as they welcome
winter's first fall of snow.
Be careful, boy, you're walking on ice.
You may fall and hurt your pride.
Crammed buses pass me by and filthy words I let fly.
While up and down I pace the street to warm my cold and tired feet.
Ah, here comes one with a little room.
Hurriedly I board it; glad to be among warm company where
Black and White rub shoulder to shoulder, forgetting for a
while the question of color.

Barbers

They are some of the most influential people
you could ever meet.
They are unsung heroes of our society.
I can remember every single one of my barbers.
The first real barber I recall is Mr. Harry.
He and his wife, Miss Enid, lived on Tenth Street,
with two sons, Kennedy and Christopher.
Either my mother or grandmother cut my baby plaits,
but they weren't real barbers.

Mr. Harry was a qualified, part-time barber.
He used to trim on Sundays in his gallery or in
the yard when the weather was fine.
Mr. Harry and I used to converse.
No baby talk, serious man to man discussion.
All through elementary school, he inquired about
my progress with genuine interest and encouragement.
I respected and trusted Mr. Harry.

My barbers are the only people I would allow to go
near my neck with a white-handled razor.
What! Can you imagine your barber going beserk with
you in his chair?
Mr. Harry, Kenneth Forde, Raymond, Bootoo, Edwin
and Barry poured positive thoughts in my head.
Barbers have to be versatile to retain their customers.
A barber wears many hats: therapist, philosopher, politician,
historian, lawyer, comedian, listener, gossiper, informant,
confidant, artist, stylist and businessman, to name a few.

I like my barbers because they always make me feel good.
Inside and outside.
Barbers make me look sharp, and feel rejuvenated.
The barbershop is like an established institution of learning.
So let's tip our hats and say a hearty:
"Thank You" to all our barbers for their significant contributions to a complex world.

Empathy

Empathy, walking a mile in the shoes of another.
Boy, Sunday ah really experience de full meaning ah dat word.
De wife fall sick wit belly pain.
Yuh know how dem woman does take in sometimes, nah.
Only dis time it was more serious.
Ah had tuh call doctah an ting.
As man, ah was real frighten.
Wen ah see de woman doublin up in pain on de floor;
She face pale, pale, pale;
An she skin cold, cold, cold;
Plus vomiting an ting;
Ah call fuh expert help.

Well boy, ah take over de household chores fuh de day.
So was later fuh football an limin in Boys High ground.
After breakfast ah start tuh cook an wash.
Even wit de washin machine, it take some skill tuh manage dem two tasks.
Yes, maco, we buy ah washer an ah dryer.
Is ah good ting ah didn't have tuh contend wit dat laundromat scene, ah woulda surely dead.

Well, Marge force an sort out de clothes.
Den she tell meh how tuh operate de machine.
Wen ah set dat up, ah start in de kitchen.
Well, yuh know yuh boy very good in de cookin section.
I eh fraid dat at all.
Wenever I cook on ah Sunday, ah does come out in ah big way.

Hear meh menu: fried rice, callaloo, stew chicken, chow mein, steak, tossed salad an Tropicana orange juice.
From ten o'clock tuh three o'clock ah shiftin meh body between cookin an washin, answerin de doorbell an telephone, carryin juice or someting fuh de sick, an once ah had tuh run by de grocery tuh buy ah papers an some Uncle Ben rice.
Add tuh dat de number ah times ah wash up wares because I is one ah dem cook dat does use ah lot ah utensils.
Wen ah done cook, ah set de table, fix mehself ah good drink, an call de wife.
Den we siddong, give thanks tuh God an start tuh eat.
Marge clear down ah small mountain like one ah Mootilal bulldozer, even though she say she wasn't feelin hungry.
Ah say, "Good, she gettin better."
Wen she done eat, she say,
"Hon, ah enjoy de food. Ah feelin better awready.
Leave de wares fuh later. Come go an relax."
Ah was very thankful fuh dat invitation because, as man, by dat time all over meh body was hurtin meh.
From dat Sunday ah had greater appreciation fuh de role of ah woman.
Three cheers fuh all women.

Good Parenting

It eh have no substitute fuh good parentin. In my boyhood days, we had several parents. First yuh had yuh real parents, yuh mudder an fadder, an den ah ton load ah family: grandparents, uncles, aunts, godparents, and cousins. In addition tuh yuh teachers an any adults. Any ah dose people coulda teach yuh de straight an narrow path which sometimes meant cuttin yuh tail.

Today, wen I hear dem talk bout corporal punishment in de schools an chirren rights, ah does want tuh laugh.
My mother an some ah dem teachers woulda surely make ah jail if dem laws was in existence den.
Rampey must be does turn in he grave wen he hear dem talkin bout chirren pushin drugs in school an bringin guns tuh class.
Two man rat cyar live in de same hole.
In Rampey school it had only one Man Rat.
Dat was Evans T. Rampersad.
He was ah model head-teacher: loved, feared an respected.
Ah remember one day Rampey spot ah fella movin after de second whistle blow.
In Barataria E.C. dat was ah cardinal sin.
De rule was once yuh hear dat second blast yuh had tuh freeze; stop watever yuh doin an wait fuh de third whistle tuh run an line up.
If yuh up in de air, stay dey like Michael Jordan.

Wen school call, Rampey call de boy up on de stage; ring de silence bell; an start tuh gi de boy ah long speech bout obeyin rules an regulations and de consequences of disobeyin.

Dat was one ting wit dem longtime teachers an parents.
Dey love tuh speechify like ah Midnight Robber before dey bus lash in yuh tail.
Sometimes de lecture was more painful an embarrassin dan de blows itself.
Yuh use tuh feel like sayin, "Awright, Rampey, cut out de set ah talk an gimme de two lash, nah."
But yuh did know better.
Except meh cousin, Cowie.
One day Rampey was goin tuh beat him.
In front de whole school, Rampey, pointin de rod at Cowie, say, "Children, there is a fool at the end of this cane."
Cowie wit he smart self arsk him, "Which end, Sir?"
Some ah de teachers an de big students start tuh giggle.
Rampey get vex an he gi Cowie four good lash on he bamsee.
Cowie start tuh break dance one time.

Yes man, rappin an all dem kinda new dance eh really new, nah.
All dem teachers an parents from long ago use tuh rap too bad.
Yuh remember yuh mudder sayin:
"Dis is goin tuh hurt me more dan it hurt you.
How many times ah have tuh tell yuh not tuh do dat, eh?
Like broomstick break in yuh ears or wat?
Well, if yuh cyar hear, yuh go feel."
Wap! Wap!
"Oh gawd, Mammy. I eh go do it again."
Wap! Wap!
All dis time yuh dancin too bad, breaksin de blows an beggin pardon. Boy, dem days was someting else. Longtime parents didn't "Spare the rod and spoil the child."
No way.
Yuh tink is de Surgeon General warning dat preventin me from smokin today.
Nah man.

Dat too abstract.
Ah remember de time wen ah pick up meh grandfadder
cigarette butt in de yard an went in de latrine.
If yuh see meh puffin away like a starboy ah see in one ah dem
twelve-thirty movie.
Ah was tryin tuh make ah smoke ring wen suddenly de door fly
open.
Ah throw de butt in the latrine pit as meh grandmudder
register ah lash on meh back.
An dash out the outhouse wit Grandma in hot pursuit;
peltin belt dat was whizzzin pass meh ears, like how dem motor-
car does speed pass one anodder on de highway.
Voosh, Voosh.
An she speechifyin too, "Yuh playin chimney.
Take dat. Go inside an take up ah book.
An doh come outside until I say so."
Dat is ah more tangible message tuh me dan some fine print
sayin: "Cigarette smoking may be dangerous to your health."

Is dem kinda parents de world need today in de fight against de
evil vices.
Strong parents; loving parents.
Parents who eh fraid ah dey own chirren.
Parents like do ones Bill Cosby describe in one ah he comedy
routines.
Parents who say, "I brought you into this world and I ain't afraid
to take you out."
Yes man, longtime parents communicated dat message loud and
clear.
My generation received it without interference or static.
Roger. Ten four.

Yuh Tink It Easy

Yuh tink it easy tuh teach in ah school witout water?
"Three years, boy!
Buh how yuh stan dat?
Is it really ah fact dat deposits in toilets remained intact to form unsightly, offensive mountains?"

Washin hands is out.
Not even ah drop tuh wet yuh mout.
Talk bout deplorable wukkin conditions.
Dust an more dust.
Make we want tuh cuss.

"Man, yuh choopid or wat?
Write letter tuh de Ministry,
Appeal fuh some salvation,
Invite dem tuh view de "splendid working conditions."

Good idea, boy!
Letters upon letters go forth
An acknowledgements return.
Open dem excitedly, hopefully. . .
O Lawd, another empty promise.
Result—enless frustration point of saturation.
Follow de pattern man.
Yuh cyar see see dat is de new scene.
Agitate and demonstrate.
Doh care bout victimize; criticize.
Confront de administration; forget de ineffective guys,
Mere glorified messengers; each wantin not to offend,

Not tuh stick his neck out.
Why? Why?
Dey fraid fuh dey present position.
Or secure at de top,
Dey scorn de cries of de little people.
So little people get up an fight.
It's your right.
Enuff of yuh scruntin an beggin.
No one will do yuh fightin.
Therefore, right now I say unite.
Better days are coming.

The Last Wicket

Six runs to go. Last pair at the wicket. Shadows lengthening. Atmosphere charged with excitement. Imminent defeat or victory for either side. That was the situation when the captain tossed the ball to me to bowl the last over of the day, and hopefully win the match for the BOOBS LANE BOYS.

The scene was the usual Sunday evening cricket match that the neighbourhood boys enjoyed back in the early sixties. That day we had invited The Tenth Street Boys to play a game on our home turf, Boobs Lane, named after one of our most unforgettable players. Boobs Lane was the unpaved section of Second Avenue, Barataria. Twelfth Street crossed it at right angles.

Our "Queens Park Oval" had never looked lovelier. All week we had worked hard preparing the pitch and surroundings for Sunday's game. Drains had been cleared; tall bushes had been levelled; and the pitch had been swept, watered and rolled. Everything was in perfect shape for keen rivalry.

Indeed the contest was very close at that point, as I stood contemplating the tremendous responsibility that was thrust upon me. At first, I almost turned down the captain's order. I said to myself, "O Lawd, why me?" Was it because I had been the most successful bowler on the team. Or did Jallo really believe that I could pull off a victory. If the Tenth Street Boys could score only six runs off me, I would have to bear picong for a week and the brunt of the blame for my side's defeat. On the other hand, what if I could get the last wicket?
All our rivals needed for victory was a good "HARRY" and it

would be all over for us. A "HARRY" was a ball struck into Mr. Harry's enclosed yard. It earned the batsman six runs and a proud walk back to the pavilion, Pa Elton's blacksmith shop. Even though a "Harry" meant instant dismissal, it was always a pleasure to clout an opposing bowler by Mr Harry. The sound of iron-beating and your team-mates shouting in unison, "Harry, Harry" as the ball sailed over the wire fence was sweet music to the ear.

Earlier in the match, there had been one "Harry". It was a real beauty that caused the lane to resound with applause and laughter. Boobs, our unpredictable, number eight batsman, had swung lustily at an overpitched ball. For a long time the air was filled with jeering and cheering as the ball descended into Mr Harry's yard. Then, suddenly, another reality dawned on the players. Silence reigned. Minds began clicking. Different strategies to obtain our ball were examined. Climbing over the fence and getting past five fierce dogs did not appeal to anyone. Distracting the dogs at one end of the yard and having someone sneak over the fence seemed quite workable, but nobody would volunteer to undertake the mission. There seemed to be only one solution; go directly up to Mr Harry's gate and politely request the ball. It had worked before. Why not now?

Retrieving the ball was always a comical scene. The group of respectful, innocent-looking players congregated in front of Mr Harry's galvanized-iron gate. Each man respected the sign: "BEWARE OF THE BARD DOGS". It was no laughing matter for at that very moment the five ferocious pothounds were fighting among themselves. They wanted to devour our only flannel ball.

On seeing that, the group quickly addressed Mr. Harry's house in voices fit for any choir, "Good evening Mr. Harry. Yuh could gi we de ball, please?" After about four pleas, an irate Mr. Harry, in a dingy, see-through jersey covering his protruding stomach, appeared at the front door of his small house. Complaining that a poor man couldn't take a rest in peace even on Sundays, Mr. Harry started to curse and threatened to "bun up de dam ball; throw it in de latrine hole and call de police." We started to beg in unison again: "Please, Mr. Harry. We wouldn't let it happen again. We promise."

At that point, the more reasonable Mrs. Harry emerged from the living-room and appealed to her husband's better judgement. She moved surprisingly fast despite her enormous size. In a flash, she was at his side and begged him, "Harry, gi de boys an dem dey ball, nah. Yuh want dem tuh stone dong de house again?" Interrupted for a while by his wife's sound reasoning, Mr. Harry hesitated in carrying out his threats. Ma Harry quickly snatched the ball from her husband's pudgy hand. She ran a few yards; her large breasts swaying left and right, up and down, with Mr. Harry in hot pursuit, and threw the ball awkwardly over the fence.

A chorus of hypocritical "Tank yuh, Miss Harry" went up from the happy group. However, the barrage of "Tank Yous" was interrupted by Ranny, the smallest member in the side. In a high-pitched voice, he shouted, "Yuh did bong tuh gi we doh."

Delivery number one and every fieldsman is on his toes: Sample, a fine wicketkeeper, is crouched behind Miss. Maude's two rusty pitchoil tins; Boobs, Gimmick, Shark, Moses, Natty, Shorty, Features, Jamesey, Chubby, Ranny and Jallo are all well-placed. I, Jamie, have the soaked flannel ball ready to knock down those pans. I let fly a scorching out-swinger. The batsman flashes outside the offstump and misses. Sample dives and collects in style. He receives an appreciative round of applause from the players and spectators.

As I contemplate my second delivery, Turkey surveys the field, crouches, blocks up the whole wicket and knocks his bat nervously on the pitch. Now, Turkey is a much respected vooper, so I have to be extra careful. Down the leg side whizzes my second ball. Turkey swings viciously but fails to connect. Once again Sample collects beautifully. Tenth Street Boys accuse me of "hidin de ball". In reply I shout "All yuh must be tink ah choopid, nah. Yuh tink I want ah Harry."

For my third ball, I extend my run-up and adjust my field. The batsmen hold a conference in the middle of the pitch; their bats clutched under their arms and their heads close together like real first-class, test match cricketers. When the batsman returns to his crease, I smile to myself as I come thundering in.

An anxious Turkey slashes dangerously at a ball that just misses the edge of the wicket by about an inch. He gets a thin outside edge. Unfortunately, the ball slips through Boobs' eager hands. He receives a round of fatigue: "Butter Fingers, Hoola-Hoop hands, Papa Lazybones." Meanwhile the batsmen cross for a well-run single.

With three balls and five runs to go, Dr. Crippins comes down to face the music. He is the number eleven batsman so I figure he is a "fish". But even "fish" could surprise you under these conditions. So I can't underrate Crippins. I decide to try a stiff, straight ball. My heart is pounding hard as I smell victory for my team. Up I come, aiming straight for his big toe and deliver right on target. It's unbelievable. The "Fish" plays a perfect, defensive stroke, right out of the books. His teammates are jubilant and shout, "No. No."

Enraged by such humiliation, I hurry back to my mark and toss down the fastest delivery of my life. My fifth ball is like greased lightning and just barely misses the wicket. Both batsman and wicketkeeper fail to detect it. Such speed. Ranny at long stump fields cleanly and returns before the batsmen could even think about running a bye.

Now it's ball number six. The last ball in the game and the outcome still hangs in the balance. Both teams confer to plan the final attack. As I stand in the cluster with my colleagues, I vaguely hear them offering all kinds of advice. I wonder how many types of balls they expect me to bowl with only one delivery. For fear of being confused by the barrage of expert tips, I totally block out all external noises and voices.

As I return to my mark, I weigh the odds. Five runs for a Tenth Street victory. One wicket would do the trick for the Boobs Lane Boys. The odds are dead even. I decide to deliver another straight ball. The air is charged with expectancy as I turn and begin my run-up. Those still able to speak offer last-minute advice, "Hit him by Harry. Knock dong de pans. Block up de whole wicket."

Me, I pray not to be struck a dreaded Harry. Dr. Crippins drags his hands in the dirt; rubs them together and grips the handle of the broad-blade bat. "O Gawd, de fella mean bizness. Help meh." That is the final prayer I utter as I aim for the rusty strip of pitchoil cans barely visible between bat and legs.

To this day, I can't remember whether my eyes were open at the actual point of delivery. All I know is that my ears did not deceive me. They instantly picked up the sweetest and most joyful sound I have ever heard: "BAM!"

Bam!

Celebrities

Barataria had its share of celebrities too, in all areas.
In mas we had bandleaders like Cito Velasquez an
Gerald Viera.
Dem was great wirebenders dat use tuh bring some
good mas.
Talk bout imagination an creativity.
Dem fellas was someting else.
Yuh remember de time Cito play Fruits An Flowers?
De tambran look so real dat yuh mout start tuh run water.
On Second Street an First Avenue, it had ah fella
name Cecil Celestine.
Slammer say he had de biggest box-cart in San Juan.
One year Cecil an Clyde Audain rock town wit ah mas
call Tiger Worshippers.
Up tuh now wen ever we meet we does still talk bout dat band.
In calypso we had plenty representatives.
We had Lord Blakie.
Ah tink he use tuh live in El Socorro but dat close enough.
He was one ah de sharpest dressin calypsonians tuh ever hit de stage.
Everybody could remember he wicked laugh an he conductin straw.
"Maria" an "Steelband Clash" was two of his greatest hits.
De most successful calypsonian had tuh be Calypso Rose.
Ah know she from since ah small.
Cathy, as we use tuh call she den, use tuh live right nex door tuh we by Miss Robbie, she aunt.
She did always like tuh sing kaiso, so was no big surprise tuh we wen she win de crown an Road March one year.

Ah remember de days wen Sparrow an some other calypsonians use tuh come by Rose.
In dem days de Birdie had he hair slick an he use tuh drive ah sleek, maroon Opel Kapitan.
Me an meh frens use tuh stand an admire de car.
Sparrow was always friendly tuh we.
In politics we had plenty representative too.
De first one ah remember is Robert E. Wallace.
He had ah drugstore at de corner ah Sixth Avenue and Fourth Street.
Wallace was from de community.
He use tuh sponsor de football league in Barataria Savannah fuh years.
An everybody in de neighborhood use tuh buy in Wallace Drugstore.
Ah remember ah time wen ah did get ah nail jook.
Wallace heself put on de heal-an-draw plaster.
Wallace had two nice daughters, Janice an Patsy.
Like all dem bizness owners had nice daughters.
Check it out man, it had de Soo Hons, de Chanasings
Chin Fatts, O'Boulands an de Rampersads.
Me an meh pardners always wanted ah girlfren wit ah shop or ah store.
Perhaps dat is wey de desire fuh ah woman wit straight hair originate.
In addition, all dem bizness people chirren use tuh do good in school.
Ah bet it have ah high correlation between bizness ownership an academic success.

Ah remember wen Wallace run fuh election in 1956.
He was ah PNM.
An dey beat up de POPPG an all dem odder independents.
People was fed up wit de likes of McNish, Albert Gomes and A.P.T. James.
Dey wanted new blood.

Who could forget Kamal?
He was ah favorite, ah real down-tuh-earth politician representin he constituents.
Ah mean yuh coulda go an see Kamal at his home in Mohammed Ville, El Socorro, on Saturday mornin.
Kamal would come out in home clothes: ah short pants an merino an ah slipper, an listen tuh yuh problem.
Den Monday mornin, bright an early, yuh could pass by he office in town an get ah letter tuh help yuh get ah wuk.
Tuh besides de man coulda talk too bad.
An yuh know how Trinidadians an Tobagonians like talkers.

Barataria had world-class athletes too.
Most notable was Christopher Forde.
One year he win ah international body-building competition.
Ah tink it was Mr. Universe.
Den we had Fitzroy Hoyte, de cyclist from Third Avenue, near Himalaya Club.
He use tuh give Roger Gibbon some real pressure.
In national football, we had Gwenwyn Cust.
He was ah nippy, lil forward dat use tuh play fuh Ball Dribblers an de famous Colts from Belmont.
Yorke and Fermin coulda ride motorbike too bad.
Dey use tuh do all kinda magic in Barataria Savannah.
All de boys use tuh drag dey foot wen dey makin ah corner on dey skater or bicycle.
Yes man, Barataria wasn't easy, nah.
We proud ah we contribution tuh de rich fabric of Trinidad and Tobago life.

Indian Food

Aye, hear nah man, if yuh want tuh eat some good Indian food, yuh have tuh eat in ah Indian weddin.
De kind dey use tuh have in Barataria.
Ah talkin from experience.
I grow up in Barataria an it had plenty Indian.
So during mango season, almost every Sunday yuh coulda find ah weddin tuh beat.
If it was close tuh home, de whole family woulda get ah formal invitation, an we woulda buy ah gift.
If it was far away, we woulda hear de music an follow we ears.

On Sunday de whole side woulda come out tuh bat.
We use tuh use terms from cricket tuh describe eatin in ah Indian weddin.
"How de bowlin goin?" mean how dey servin de food; heavy or light.
"How much innings yuh bat?" mean how much time yuh eat.

Indian food on baliser leaf is de greatest.
After all de invited guests eat was time fuh me and meh side tuh take de field: long wooden tables an benches set up under ah bamboo tent covered wit coconut branch or galvanize.
Fus ting was de leaf. Den was de rice.
De man would put rice until yuh tell him, "Stop."
Den yuh had tuh make ah crater in de mountain ah rice.
In dat he would pour ah ladle ah dahl, puree split peas.
Nex was de buss-up shut an de curry mango.
Dat was my favorite combination, my kinda bowlin.
If dey had curry channa or pumpkin talcarie was en'less boundary.

Mankind had tuh loosen dey belt.
Boy, eatin dat food wid yuh fingers was de sweetest ting.
It was hot an spicy.
Pepper was no problem because it had plenty water.
Yes, eatin real Indian food does leave yuh wit some warm memories.
All day Monday use tuh be tears.
But nobody didn't care because come nex Sunday we lookin fuh anodder match.

In Indian weddin we use tuh run competition tuh see who could eat de most.
See who was de number one batsman.
On we side dat honor went tuh two brothers, Sharko an Bullface.
Dem fellas coulda eat too bad.
Wat we couldn't eat we use tuh put in brown paper bag an carry home fuh de rest ah de family.
Was ah kinda bribe fuh wen we stay out too late.
Yuh tink it easy, nah.

Aye, hear nah man, ah eat in all kinda four-star Indian restaurant in Trinidad an even San Francisco.
An believe meh, none ah dem could beat back de food in any Trinidad-Indian weddin.
We Indian is de best Indian cooks in de world.

Family Gathering

There is something special about family members gathered in a bedroom.
Some lying, some sitting on the bed or on the floor and some standing.
The last time we did that was a few weeks ago after my step-father's death.
It was like birds returning to their nest.
To be together, to cry, to sing, to laugh, to touch.
To talk with words and without words;
To reminisce, to love, and just to be.
There was Mammy, a widow now,
Monica, the first-born,
Doreen, Ashley, Paula and Rodney;
And Doreen's two children, Maria and Brent.
It was like if we were taking a head count to confirm the physical absence of our dear dad, Ivan George.
May he rest in peace.
It was also a time for us to reflect on our lives.
Where have we been?
Where are we now?
And where are we going?
And most important, who is taking us there.
Yes, death can be a powerful teacher, if only we let it.
It does not discriminate.
Death equalizes everybody in the end.
Creed, color, class and race is of no account in the sight of God.
Each one stands on his own merit.
The family is, in fact, the primary group.
Let's nurture and preserve it.
It's the strength of our foundation.

The Man

In America wen yuh say "The Man," yuh referrin tuh de white man.
In Trinidad an Tobago, it eh so at all.
We does add on man tuh de end of ah word tuh tell yuh wat de man does do fuh ah livin or wat kinda man he is.
Fuh example, de obeahman.
Yuh remember him?
In Africa de whiteman call him "Witch Doctor," de man who does wuk black magic tuh get yuh watever or whoever yuh want.
Den dey have de whe-whe man.
He was de forerunner of de National Lottery.
But he was illegal.
Yuh tink it easy.

Every village have ah sweetman, de Village Ram.
Dat is de man who have plenty woman, doh wuk noway, always lookin sharp an have chirren all over de place.
On de odder hand, yuh have de hard-wukkin bottlesman, pushin he cart in de hot sun, buyin people empty bottle an sellin dem tuh Fernandes Distillery.
Ah remember him good because we use tuh tief he bottles an sell dem back tuh him.
While one man sellin him some rum bottles way in de back ah de yard, anodder two in de front helpin deyself in he cart.
We use tuh be considerate though.
Take jus enough tuh go twelve-thirty by Ritz Cinema an buy ah bread an curry channa an ah red Solo by Ramdeen Snackette.
Boydays was plenty fun.
Ah remember one mornin de milkman fall dong wit about ah

hundred bottle on he bike.
If yuh see mas.
Nylon, de fishman, was cleanin ah carite fuh Miss Robbie.
He throw de fish guts in de road, an bout ten pothound start tuh fight.
If yuh see ruckshun.
Two ah dem bounce Bajnath front wheel an he catspraddle.
Yuh talk bout milk an broken bottle: green bottle, brown bottle, clear bottle; bottle of all shapes an sizes.
Nylon apologize tuh Bajnath, an we went an help him up.

Longtime de steelbandman was ah real social outcast.
He an de calypsonian.
Yuh see how tings change today.
In dem days, no mudder wanted dey son tuh go near ah panyard or sing kaiso.
Much less see dey decent, self-respectin daughter talkin tuh ah steelbandman or ah calypsonian.
Yuh want yuh mudder kill yuh or wat?

Longtime, like every man had ah role an responsibility.
It had de preacherman, icecream-man, iceman, papersman, paletman, taximan, policeman, fireman, teacherman, waterwoman, garbageman and de sharpman.
Yuh remember de good-fuh-nutten man?
In dis modern world, some ah dem man disappearin.
Dat is progress, dey say.
Ah glad ah had de chance tuh know dem man an dem.

De Rasquelles

Front Row: Marjorie Foster, Janice McEwen, Pat Forde, Yvonne Williamson
Back Row: June Rodney, Velma Smith, Marilyn Billy, Jean Holligam, Gemma Ferguson

De Rascals

Front row: Gordon Bennett, Rodney Foster, Raymond Ferguson
Back row: Anthony Williamson, Hubert Liverpool, Jeffrey Gibson, George Rodney

Gone But Not Forgotten

Some called him Charlo, The General, Trail, The Hammer
Most of his friends called him Rudolph.
I called him Rudolph.
From the day I first met him face to face there was instant admiration and respect, as I sat amazed looking at him tune a tenor pan.
I considered him a genius; the consummate artist; a leader among men; a man with a vision, a brave man, a national treasure and hero; a man with a dream.
And like every other dreamer, he had a deep fear.
Fear that one day "The Man go tief we ting".

Yes, Rudolph feared that one day the white man would capitalize on our indigenous art form; the most innovative musical instrument of the twentieth century, the steelpan, the pan, an instrument and a type of music that Rudolph dedicated his life to improving, taking it to Mother Africa, London, The United States of America and Canada.

One evening, in Inglewood, California,
Our hero and friend shared that fear with me, thousands of miles from his beloved Laventille Hills in Trinidad.
He reminded me of the prophet who was not honored in his own country.
Rudolph wondered when the Government and the people with the money would start doing more for pan.
When they would start "puttin dey money wey dey mout is".

Nowadays, as I read the daily papers, there is confirmation that his prophecy is being fulfilled.
What are we going to do?
When are we going to stop the talking and start "de action".
Did Rudolph and his predecessors labor in vain?
Did they die in vain?
No, my fellow Trinbagonians.
Let's honor our national heroes and invest in pan.
Move steelband to a higher ground.
Come on my fellow Brothers and Sisters.
Don't let them steal pan from right under our noses.
Is we ting, keep it; treasure it; love it.
Doh disappoint Spree and Rudolph and all the pioneers of pan.
Let's do something constructive, otherwise **The Man** will certainly steal it.
Is it too late?

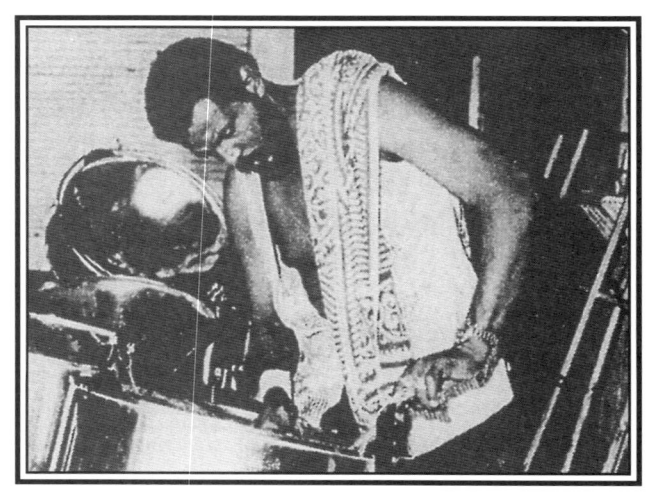

Photo: Courtesy of Carol Charles, wife.

Rudolph Charles, captain of Desperados

Desire

Man, I want tuh play ah pan so bad, eh.
Ah really cyar describe it.
Ah want tuh beat one ah Rudolph Charles double-tenor wit de
skill an sweetness of Robert Greenidge, Earl Rodney, Boogsie
Sharpe an Ken " Professor" Philmore combined.
Dat go be sweet pan.
Ah go be de hardest panman in de land.
Den some days ah does want tuh beat ah six-bass,
so dat ah could real gallery mehself.
Yuh know how dem bassmen does show orf.
If yuh see meh strikin dem notes all behine
meh back witout even lookin.
Ah like dat too bad.
Ah want tuh be as hard as meh pardner Barry from
Solo an Pops from Hylanders.
Yuh remember dem fellas.
Dey was bad fuh days.
Den again ah like de trap-set man, de drummer.
Yuh remember Toby Tobias from Despers an de
fella from Fonclaire?
Well, I want tuh be just like dem, breakin dong
de place wit meh constant tempo.
Ah go have de whole ah town bawlin fuh more.
Wen ah tired wit dat, ah want tuh beat some iron.
Steelband music must have ah good rhythm section.
So ah want tuh beat iron like meh brother, Hanny,
an he fren, Cory.
Dem is de sweetest iron men ah ever hear.
If yuh hear meh: Ah-nock-he-dong, Ah-nock-he-dong,

Ah-nock-he-dong.
Clang, Clang, Clang, Clang.
An ah want tuh scratch too.
Like de scratcherman, Leiba, from Tripoli.
Dat fella coulda scratch, boy.

After ah get all hot an excited an ah want tuh cool dong,
Ah go play some cello an guitar pan.
Ah go be strummin an pullin some sweet chords.
Dat go have de whole band chippin an dancin.

Yes man, ah want tuh be ah real talented panman;
able tuh play in all de different section.
Pan is de greatest.
An ah playin from kaiso tuh classic.
Ah versatile too bad.
So Santa, all yuh boy want fuh Christmas
Is ah sweet tenor pan an ah go be very, very happy.

Sundays

I remember Sundays as special days in Trinidad and Tobago. There is a kind of reassuring feeling about Sunday. It was a feeling that seemed to say that everything was going to be all right. Probably it was because most people prayed on Sundays.

On Sunday, we went to church to pray and give thanks for God's many blessings during the past week and to ask Him to watch over us in the days ahead. In my boyhood days, I went to Sunday school at St Colombo's Anglican Church in Barataria. In those days Rev. Silman was the minister. Some of the Sunday school teachers used to teach at school too, Barataria E.C. I enjoyed attending Sunday school. I liked to hear those Bible stories and answer questions. Sometimes the teacher would give prizes. My friends and I used to enjoy singing hymns like "All Things Bright And Beautiful." Now and then we used to slip in our own musical arrangement. We were among the first to introduce pan in church, with our mouths and voices.

Sunday also provided another opportunity to play with my schoolmates who I hadn't seen since Friday evening. We had to be careful not to get too sweaty or dirty our clothes, our Sunday best. The worse thing was to get a licking on Sunday. You would be cursed for the rest of the week. Sunday school also meant witholding some of yuh money fuh collection. Ah mean who go miss yuh penny. Tuh besides de lady in Fly Parlor use tuh have fresh curry mango and pepper tambran on Sundays. Before we reach home we had tuh make sure dat we wash away all de evidence of stopping by de parlor. Yuh shoulda see we by de stanpipe.

Ah could still remember meh mudder sayin, "Come inside an take meh clothes off yuh back. An take meh Bata four ninety-five off yuh foot." Yes man, dem clothes an shoes wasn't really yours, nah. Dey jus len yuh tuh go tuh church an come back.

It still amazes me wen I recall dat regardless of how bad tings was, it always had food in de house on Sundays. Perhaps dat is why Sunday is so special fuh me. Ah really cyar remember being hungry on ah Sunday in Trinidad. During de week yes, but never on ah Sunday.

As ah matter ah fact, Sunday was good food day. Good food mean meat, callaloo and crab, macaroni pie, red beans, rice, plantain, watercress and lettuce, beets and juice. Of course, it had Sundays and Sunday. Ah Sunday wit Soursop or Peanut Punch different from one wit lime juice or koolaid. Come on man, if yuh from dose times yuh know exactly wat ah talkin bout.

One ah de sweetest sounds yuh could hear on ah Sunday is wen yuh mudder throw de meat in de iron pot tuh brown. Shrah, Shrah. Dat is ah excitin, promisin sound. De number ah shrahs yuh hear could tell yuh how much meat dey cookin. Is roughly two shrahs tuh ah pound ah meat. In our yard, at Sixty-seven Tenth Street, Barataria, it use tuh have plenty shrahs. It was shrahs from Cousin Baby, Cousin Yvonne, Nenny Nica and meh mudder, Frances. Sometimes wen dey cook different tings dey use tuh trade. Boy, Nenny coulda stew ah duck. Sweet tuh de bone. Yes man, on Sundays people use tuh be more Christian- like.

Sundays also meant de day wen meh mudder would teach we tuh eat wit knife an fork, an how tuh set de table wit de Sunday wares. My mudder had hope an vision. She say we had tuh learn proper etiquette so dat we would be ready wen we make it in de world. She didn't want we tuh make she shame wen we went to other people house or move up in society. Ah could still hear she sayin, "Sit properly and take yuh elbows orf de table." Thank you, Mammy. I love you. Parents long ago had ah ting against chirren making dem shame. Dey would kill yuh fuh doin dat.

On Sundays, we use tuh tell time by listening tuh special programs on de radio or Redifusion. Yuh could remember de Sam Ghany show? Dat was fun. An, of course, who could forget Auntie Kay and Uncle Bob, an de Dawlett Ahee band. Ah could still remember one ah de theme songs, "Dandy Candy, I am feeling hungry. After lunch or tea, gimme ah piece ah Dandy Candy." Thanks tuh all dem sponsors like Jaleel Bottling Works and Red Spot, Ju-c and Cannings, and Uncle A.M. Querino for makin my childhood a most enjoyable and memorable experience.

As a grown man, I still look forward to the revitalizing qualities of Sundays. Sunday is like a rebirth; an opportunity to start anew. I still go to church on Sundays wherever I am and give thanks to the Lord for bringing me through the past week. I ask for His guidance during the days ahead. I thank Him for family, friends, and neighbours, far and wide. I like the sun in Sunday because it brightens my life with the promise of God's abundant goodness.

Good Friday

It have days wen ah Trinidadian does cook an odder days wen he does jus cook.
Wey is de difference?
Every true, true Trini know dat cooking on Good Friday, Easter, Carnival an Christmas different from cooking on any odder days.
If yuh still in doubt an pretendin yuh doh know wat ah talkin bout, jus arsk meh pardner, John D.
He go tell yuh wat ah mean.

Fuh example, today is Good Friday.
Tuh begin wit, me ain't wukkin noway.
Good Friday is ah Holy Day, ah special day in de Christian religion.
Since ah small, I accustom doin certain tings on dis day.
Like goin tuh church, eatin hot crossbuns an eatin ah traditional Good Friday meal.
Good Friday is fish, preferably salt salmon, salt mackrel or saltfish.
We use tuh have dat wit ground provision: dasheen, yam, sweet potato an cassava, an some plantain an green fig.
Some watercress an juice would complete de meal.

Dis year ah decide tuh cook saltfish.
Ah love saltfish too bad; more dan Sparrow.
So yesterday ah pick up two pounds ah de good saltfish; bacallo, four ninety-nine ah pound.
Today, ah take over de kitchen.
I cookin de food.
Wen I go in de kitchen, ah doh want no audience,
so meh wife does disappear tuh some odder part ah de house.

She say ah does make ah mess ah de kitchen wen ah cookin.
Ah explain tuh she dat wen I come out tuh cook me eh bizness wit cleanin.
Cookin an cleanin is two different ting tuh me.
Wen I man creatin meh pot, ah cyar bother meh
head wit wipin down stove an all dem set ah nonsense.

Meh menu today is ground provision, dumplin, stew saltfish wit whole baby ochro, an ah cucumber wit sweet pepper an tomato salad.
Yes, ah have good sweet oil too.
On Good Friday yuh have tuh cook wit nuff olive oil an plenty onion.
Ah didn't always like olive oil, but over de years I have acquired a taste for it.
After about two hours, ah finish meh creation an ah call meh wife.
"Aye, Marge, come an get it while it hot."
She eat like ah viking, den she tell meh,
 "Yuh eh lose yuh touches."
Ah smile an say, "Thanks."

My Kitchen Table

I owe a great deal to my kitchen table
For I have spent many hours there, either eating or studying.
I find it the most relaxing and productive place to do my studying and writing.
As soon as the dishes were cleared, I took over.
Even today, although I have a room designated as my study, I still find myself drawn to my reliable, old kitchen table.
There is an unbreakable bond between my Kitchen Table and me.
Not even my wife can break it, try as she may.
Every time she removes my stuff to the study, I return them the next day.
My Kitchen Table has been a silent supporter all through my academic success: elementary school, high school, college, graduate school and even now as I write my first book.
If only my friend could talk.
Boy, what stories he would tell.
He would tell you about the many, long hours we have shared together.
Some painful and tiring; but the majority enjoyable and memorable.
Therefore, Marj, next time you see my stuff on the kitchen table, don't mess with it.
He's my friend; friends have to stick together.

Callousness

This morning I was very callous as I stood and watched the old, crouched figure on the floor and did not make a move to help, or feel the least concern for her condition.
In fact, I couldn't care less.
Or perhaps I did.
But...

Man, I was late for my part-time job.
And besides there were other passengers in the carriage, one of whom had to be more qualified to react in such an emergency.
So why should I, in my ignorance, get involved.
In addition, she didn't look too clean.
One passenger shifted as the vagrant clawed the air in a vain attempt to regain her seat.
Another one moved to the next carriage.
Everyone just cast a cursory glance, as the train stopped; disgorged commuters; ingested some more; and then sped off noisily to the next stop.

As I left the scene, I questioned myself because I still didn't feel guilty or sorry about my reaction.
"Have six years in New York City eroded my emotions?," I wondered.
"Is this what it means to live, to survive, in The Big Apple? Is this civilized behavior?"
By the way, if you were in my shoes,
What would you have done?

Ups and Downs

In 1973 ah went up tuh de States tuh further meh studies so dat ah could come back down tuh Trinidad an move up in society.
Ah mean tuh say, isn't dat how all dem big boys do it?
Go up tuh London, an den come back down an be Prime Minister, an judge, an lawyer an ting.
But wen ah come down in 1980, dey say ah overqualified.
Dey eh need no Master's Degree fuh dat position.
Tuh besides dey didn't even know how tuh classify guidance counselor wit ah six-month diploma, much less one wit ah Master's in Education.
So like is best ah did stay in Morvant North an jus draw meh salary an annual increments den.
So ah get vex; an ah went back up.

Bill Trotman did joke bout dis up an down ting Trinidadians does go thru.
Is ah serious topic, oui.
Is it ah directional ting because of de position on de map or is it ah attitude?
Does up mean advanced an down mean backward?
Wat you tink, man?

Mas In Los Angeles

It was real mas in Los Angeles when Trinidad and Tobago earned a draw against the United States in an exciting soccer game in the 1990 World Cup Series. To really capture the flavor of this memorable game, I believe I have to describe the experience in true Trini dialect. No other language would be as accurate and picturesque.

From de time ah land at El Camino Stadium, ah pick up on some positive vibes. Ah hear some heavy soca comin from ah ghetto-blaster. Like magic ah was drawn tuh de music. Soca music sweet too bad. Wavin meh lil national flag, I approached de group. Ah spot ah fella name Mango leadin de section, ah big national flag in he han.

Ah know Mango playin some bad ball in Brooklyn at Boys High ground about nine years ago. Ah shout out, "Mango, weh goin orn?" After ah typical Trini greetin, ah fella in de group offer meh ah ticket. Just so. No money asked. One hundred percent free. Ah say tuh mehself, "Buh Rodney, how yuh lucky so? Like yuh in Trinidad or wat?" It was eider Monroe from New Mexico or Cox from Boston who gimme de ticket. Den ah recognize de fella carryin de player. It was meh pardner Ramdoo cousin, Trevor Tillett. Wat good fortune tuh fall into ah group ah fun-lovin Trinis.

We entered de stadium singin an chippin tuh de sweet sound of soca. Ah was on ah natural high. De handful ah we went round de stadium wavin we flag, singin, knockin soda cans, jinglin keys an showin de other people how we does behave wen we national team playin. In-between we was shoutin "BEAT U.S.A." Monroe, in ah true reporter's voice was forecastin de score at de end ah de first half. He predicted dat we woulda drop four on dem. Ah know alyuh know de outcome ah de game, so ah go spare all yuh de details. Wat ah want tuh recreate is de atmosphere; de Carnival mood ah de two hundred or so Trinidad and Tobago supporters. Man, though outnumbered, we sounded like angels wen we proudly sang de National Anthem. Regardless ah wat immigrant status in de U.S.A., on Saturday, May 13th, 1989, at twelve o' clock, all ah we remember wey we navel string bury.

Ah tell yuh, we kept up de tempo and jammin even though we was one down in de final minutes ah de game. We felt positive dat we could "Beat de U.S.A." Therefore, wen dat player make de cross an another one sell de whole world ah "dummy" interception, and de ball went tuh de fella who beats up some Yankees and score de goal, ah wasn't surprised one bit. Excuse meh for leavin out names. Ah leave home sixteen years now an me eh know none ah dem young boys, except "Gally" de coach.

We had appealed tuh de Gods through we drummin, iron knockin, an soca chants, and dey had smiled on us. Ah deafening roar went up wen de ball enter de net. We shout until we hoarse. We wine; we sing; we take ah drink an wave we flag; raise de volume on de tempo. "It was not ah fete again. It was madness."

Ah nice-looking, curvaceous chick who was sharin out some pelau wen de goal score shout out, "Ah could gi dat fella some pelau right now." De crowd laugh scandalously, in true Trini style. Ah fella say, "Wit de size ah pot yuh have dey, yuh could gi all ah we." More laughter.

Ah say it was mas in L.A. because it had all de ingredients of ah Carnival scene in Trinidad. People who eh see one another fuh years embraced, kissed, shake hands, exchange telephone numbers and addresses and promise tuh keep in touch. Yes, of course it had cussin. Wat, wit some ah dem calls de referee make, it did bong tuh have cussin. One fella wit ah amplified voice shout, "Aye, Ref! Referee! Yuh blind or wat? Like yuh eye bus or wat? Yuh eh see de man pullin de fella jersey?"
De section start tuh sing, "De referee is ah fowl tief. De referee is ah fowl tief."
It eh have nobody could cuss as sweet an colorful as a Trini. We is de greatest.

If yuh tink Cummings was de only coach, yuh lie. It had some loud mouth men and women shouting directions from de stands. At times yuh would hear, "Line! Line! Take ah shot! Bring him dong!. Take ah leg!" At other times we would openly acknowledge wen de USA make some good plays. We know good quality football wen we see it. Yes man, dem white boys play some bad ball too.

Wen de final whistle came, it was mas. De two rhythm sections join up and for ah long, long, long time we just jammed. Like mankind didn't want tuh let go of de moment. Sparrow's medley never sounded better. We show Americans how tuh celebrate at a football match. Dey was lookin on in amazement at how peacefully and jubilantly we enjoyed sharing de points. Ah could only imagine wat woulda happen if we did win.

Yes man, ah felt real proud of we national team, de Strike Squad. Well done fellas. See you in Rome. Saturday, May 13th., 1989, was indeed a memorable day. It was mas in Los Angeles.

Go Trinidad & Tobago Go!

Brooklyn Experience

"Brooklyn is meh home."
De Mighty Sparrow say so in "Mas In Brooklyn".
I could relate tuh dat.
Ah live eight years in Brooklyn an nex tuh Trinidad,
ah consider Brooklyn meh second home.

Ah have some solid roots in Brooklyn, man.
Wat, wit all dem family an frens ah still have livin dey,
ah love Brooklyn too bad.
Brooklyn in many ways is like Trinidad.
Did somebody say is de reverse?
Not me an dat, nah.
I eh touchin dat topic.
During de Summer, yuh could bounce up everybody
on Flatbush Avenue.
Ah does wonder who in Trinidad runnin de country.

Aye, hear nah man, dem Korean vegetable store
have everyting ah Trinidadian want.
Wat dey eh have, check out Gloria on Nostrand.
Brooklyn does have some ah de hardest fete in de world.
If yuh doubt meh, check out Tilden Hall on Labor
Day weekend.
Is Charlies Roots, Blue Ventures, Byron Lee an sometimes
Tokyo, Despers or one ah dem big steelband.
Is enless jam all over de place.
An doh talk bout basement party in de winter.
Dat is someting else, altogether.
Yuh ever hear Hanny and Lion and De Naturals jammin some

heavy soca in Kenzie an Wilma basement?
Dat is ah unforgettable experience.
Hanny is de hardest iron man ah ever meet.
Ah could still remember dancin de Grind in de dark
in de early seventies.
De Grind was de predecessor of Lambada.

Brooklyn fuh me is opportunity.
Is like ah buffet; ah smogasboard;
choose wey yuh want.
If yuh want tuh study, it have school fuh everyting.
Yuh want tuh run woman, it have plenty woman.
Ah good man still "like ah piece ah gold" in Brooklyn.
Sparrow eh lie at all.
Yuh want tuh lime, it have plenty corner, bar an club.
Yuh want tuh exercise, it have enless crowded parks.
Yes man, Brooklyn fuh me is choices.
Yuh could advance, stay stagnant, or go backward.

By de way, lemme gi yuh dis joke.
One nite ah tort ah was havin ah nightmare.
Ah was feelin hungry so ah get up an went in de kitchen.
As ah turn on de light, ah start tuh bawl.
If yuh see German roach, all different sizes.
Yes boy, Brooklyn have some super rat an roaches.
Like dey does lift weights or take steroids.
Ah was frighten because ah tort ah was in East Germany.
It was 1973, an dey didn't break dong de wall yet.
Like de roach an dem was havin ah big fete.
If yuh see how dey run fuh cover.
Ah swear some ah dem was faster dan Ben Johnson.
Fortunately, meh wife come tuh de rescue.
She produce two can ah Raid, an we start tuh spray.
If yuh see Germans we kill.

Yes man, in Brooklyn dey always tryin tuh exterminate or eliminate someting.

Mother Leon annual thanksgivin is anodder unforgettable experience.
Is Baptist thanksgivin, Trinidad style: plenty prayers, singin, bell-ringin, testifyin an, of course, plenty good food.
Daddy Leon does make ah bad sponge cake.
Yes man, every year people does come from all over tuh fellowship an give thanks.
Mankind suppose tuh give God plenty thanks wen dey livin in Brooklyn.

Ah love Brooklyn fuh its diversity.
Is ah kinda love-hate relationship.
Yuh know wat ah mean? Good.
Brooklyn is a city of contrasts:
hope an despair, war an peace;
success an failure; growth an decline;
hot an cold, friendly an hostile;
up an down, beauty an ugliness;
feast an famine, rich an poor.
Yes, Brooklyn is ah puzzle.
Is like life itself.
I like life. I love Brooklyn.

Customs In Puerto Rico

Aye, hear nah man, yuh ever check out de tings ah true, true Trini does bring back from ah trip tuh Trinidad?
De odder day yuh shudda hear meh describin tuh de customs officer in Puerto Rico.
Dis is fried King Fish, an dat is curry mango, anchar,
Dose are tambran balls, tamarino,
Dat is fry channa, garbanza beans,
An dat is mauby bark, bay leaf, sea moss, dinner mints, Golden Ray butter, kuchela, ah homemade sweetbread, pastelles, currants rolls, salt prunes, chinese plums an frozen coconut water.
Oh dat? Dat is buss-up shut an some dalphourrie tuh eat wit de curry mango.
Is someting like ah Mexican burrito.
An of course dis is homemade pepper sauce.
Every true, true, Trini must bring back some.
Right now is just pure pepper grind up wit vinegar.
Ah go add de rest ah de ingredients wen ah reach up.
Nah, Senor, dat is black cake.
Don't you dare call my mudder fruit cake no puddin.
Yuh see dis black ting here?
Dat is wat we does call puddin.
Oh, in dis bag here is de world famous Angostura Bitters an two bottle ah rum.
Yes, ah tink dat is all oui, officer.
Ah tell yuh, de day dey start tuh charge tax on all dem tings Trini does bring back, we go bawl like forty Tarzan.

Reflections

At forty thousand feet in de air.
An five hours flyin before yuh touch Mother Earth
Is plenty time an distance fuh ah man tuh reflect;
Tuh engage in some deep, deep thoughts.

De odder day on ah flight from Miami tuh Los Angeles,
Ah was engaging in some serious dialogue wit mehself.
Ah start arskin mehself some hard, hard question:
"Rodney, wey yuh goin?
Wey yuh comin from?
Wat is yuh mission in life?
Wat role yuh come out tuh play?
Wat plans de Good Lord have fuh yuh?
Flyin in any kinda plane is one ah de most trustin
relationships ah man could experience.
I eh scared ah flyin, but ah does still wonder how ah
big maco plane, weighin all dem tons, does go up,
stay up, an den come back down.
Yuh ever notice dat de sky doh have no reference points?
Flyin is not like travellin in ah maxi taxi from Port-of-Spain
tuh Arima along de Eastern Main Road.
Up in de sky eh have no flyover, Tambran Tree, Morvant Junction
Croisee, Curepe or de Dial.
Is only blue sky an white cloud wit no sign.
Of course wen dey experience some turbulence ah tort de pilot
was passin through dem pothole in Dinsely.
 Boy, dat plane start tuh shake up like ah earthquake;
or dat musta be ah skyquake.
"Fasten seat belt" sign start tuh flash.

An de captain, in ah real cool voice announce,
"Would passengers in the aisles kindly return to your seats?"
Well, me eh pay he no mind.
I had ah number tuh pass an ah jus had tuh go.
Was eider dat or ah flood down de plane.
Yes man, flyin could be ah real humblin experience.
It provides an opportunity fuh mankind tuh reflect.

Mausica

The two most memorable years of my life so far were spent at Mausica Teachers College. I entered Mausica, as it was popularly called, in September, 1966, at age 19. It seemed that I was destined to attend Mausica.

The first time that I heard about a college for training young, would-be-teachers was at Harry Joseph's home in Mt. Lambert. My good friend, Errol Williams, now deceased, and I had gone to visit Harrison Joseph, Mr Joseph's son. Errol and Harry Joe were attending St. George's College. I was going to Osmond High School in San Juan. I remember the day clearly. It was raining and we were liming in the gallery.

At some point, Harry Joe explained that his father was the principal of Mausica Teachers College. He described it as a place where high school graduates without any prior teaching experience could undergo a two-year teacher-training program. Since I had always wanted to be a teacher, I decided there and then that Mausica was the place for me.

From then on I studied hard to obtain at least five 'O'Levels, Mathematics and English Language included. In my first attempt at G.C.E, I obtained four passes: French, Spanish, Geography and Mathematics. I failed the all-important English Language. In fact, I received the lowest grade possible - a nine. My teachers couldn't understand how I could have failed English, and gained distinctions in French (1) and Spanish (2). No one sought an explanation from the Ministry or Cambridge. In those days when they say "Yuh fail." Yuh fail. It was 1965.

It was back to Osmond for another year. Kind-hearted Mr. Arthur Murray, the principal, gave me a half-scholarship. May God bless his soul. My grandmother paid three dollars and fifty cents a month.

I concentrated on English Language and Mathematics and took the exam again in June of 1966. I was confident that I would pass this time because I had promised myself that in my descriptive essay the material would be all mine. The first time I had foolishly used part of a model essay I had read the night before. I believed that was the reason why I failed.

However, even though I knew I had my pass in the bag, I faced another problem. The results of the exam would not be available before the interviews for the 1966 scholarships. What could I do? Now, as I reflect on my predicament, I have to compliment myself on how I successfully solved it.

I visited the Ministry of Education on Alexandria Street and met one Mrs. Harris, a very kind and helpful public servant. I explained to her that I would have the necessary qualifications before classes began in September, 1966, and that I would like to be interviewed. She in turn said that it wasn't possible, but there was still some hope of fulfilling my dream. Mrs. Harris explained that usually after the initial selection of the fifty-five men, a few did not accept the scholarships. A second interview was held to fill those places. I said, "Good." One of those scholarships had Rodney written all over it.

To cut a long story short; I was selected. Would you believe that I received the invitation for the interview at ten o'clock the same day of the interview. My appointment was at nine o'clock? You should have heard me pleading with the taxi-drivers from San Juan to St. James. Talk about fate and luck.

The Red Guards
Mausica Teachers College
1966-1968

Back row left to right:
Joseph Ragoonansingh, Selwyn Bethelmy, Carlsbury Gonzalez, Rodney Foster, Michael Murrell

Front row left to right:
Leroy David, Andrew Miguel, Kent Rennie, Martin Brathwaite

Mausica was a seat of great learning both academically and socially. There we were, in a new environment, two hundred and twenty young adults trying and learning to define ourselves. Mausica was a residential campus. It was the first time that many of us had lived away from home.

In my stay there, I had two fine room-mates: Leroy Cox, in my first year, and Carlsbury Gonzales, in my second year. We were like blood-brothers. In addition, I established several close friendships with staff and fellow-students.

At Mausica we laughed, we sang, we loved, we fought, we played, we prayed, we grew and we learned what it meant to be good human beings. It was a dynamic learning environment. At the helm was one of the country's most influential educators, the late Harry Joseph. He was ably assisted by a dedicated staff. Among them were Fitz-James Williams, the Warden, and Daphne Pilgrim-Cuffie, lecutrer and Dean of Women. Together they helped mould the minds of the young Mausicans.

I remember Fanny Roopchand. She taught Sociology. One statement she often repeated and which I find most profound to this day was: "Never be ashamed of your humble origin." Yes, Fanny, that was heavy.

Scratchy, now Dr. Lewis, sang about the same idea in one of his popular calypsoes. He ridiculed those students from Pt. Zagaya, deep country, who suddenly discovered that they couldn't eat yam and dasheen once they had entered Mausica. Yes, there were a few who denied their roots. Not me. I was proud of my background.

The motto at Mausica was, "When you work, work hard. When you play, play hard." Most of us adhered to it because there was a nice balance between work and play. Learning was fun and challenging. Mr. Harry Joseph and Mr. Hamlyn Dukhan used to play with our minds when they taught Philosophy and Ethics. Just when you thought you had the definitive answer, they would introduce some other point that would totally confuse you.

Going on teaching practice was an adventure. It was full of fears, promises, discoveries and excitement. Ask any Mausican about preparing notes of lessons: two long notes and a short, charts and other didactic material. Ask them how they reacted when De Joe announced in assembly that the external panel would be visiting their schools.

I could still vividly remember the fun times we used to have when we returned to campus after a long day in the classroom. Everybody wanted to be on the bus with Selwyn Beckles and Lester Wilkinson. Lester played a mean guitar and sang as well. Beck had a phenomenal memory. Do you know the song, "There was a flea. The prettiest lil flea there ever could be?" Well Beck could sing that whole song in his sleep. I was good on the chorus: "And the green grass grows all around and around. And the green grass grows all around." Chess was a very popular game at Mausica. We had our own version of the activity. I loved it immensely. Nuff said.

Yes, my two years at Mausica are indelibly etched in my mind. I will always cherish their pleasant memories.

Brother and Sister

There is something special about a brother and sister talking in the wee hours of the morning.
She sitting at the foot of the bed setting her hair, he half-lying, half-sitting on the bed.
Both trying to accept the fact that their stepfather, Ivan, is gone.
Dead, taken by a massive heart attack.
They both had known him for about thirty years
and loved him dearly, too.
Both agree he was a good man, a nice man who would be sorely missed by all.
Not too many words are spoken.
Not too many need be said.
At times like these; just being there
sharing the time and space is adequate.
This is my sister's house.
A real house: three bedrooms, two baths etc.
Now I am uncle to her two kids, Maria and Brent.
I feel good when they call me "Uncle Rod".
Pet is doing well in her job, too.
Just passed those hard Accounting exams;
one of seven people in the whole country.
Now she could put letters after her name.

With adoring eyes, I look at my baby sister;
now a mother, a friend and a successful, Black woman.
It seems like it was only yesterday that I used to take her
to school and help her with her lessons.
Is this what we dreamed about when we played dolly-house together?

She and I yawn together, laugh, and then agree,
"It's time to get some sleep.
Tomorrow is another long day."
"Wake me in the morning, dear," I say.
"Mammy and I are going to church at St Mary's.
Eight o'clock. Goodnight, Pet. Sleep well."
"You too, Rod. Goodnight."

The Seasons

Mention de word "seasons" an immediately yuh might tink bout de weather an climate.
In Trinidad an Tobago, we have two seasons: de rainy season and de dry season.
But is not dem seasons I want tuh talk bout.
I want tuh remind yuh bout seasons full of fun.
Like mango season.
Dat was meh favorite.
It use tuh coincide wit Summer vacation; mid-July tuh early September.
Was almost two months of eating mango in all shape an fashion.
First was mango chow.
We use tuh make dat wit full or half-ripe mango.
In somebody big enamel bowl or plastic bowl, we use tuh cut up mango an add salt, pepper an water.
Sometimes after ah game of cricket or pitchin marbles, we use tuh have ah feast.

Yuh remember how everybody use tuh put dey hand in de bowl?
Wen de chow done, de water use tuh be colored wit dirt.
Yuh tink dat stop we from drinkin de pepper water.
Dat was one time dat mankind use tuh forget dat Boobs use tuh suck finger.
Anyhow, we use tuh say dat de pepper an salt go kill de germs.

Yuh could do plenty tings wit mango.
Yuh remember curry mango an kuchela?
Red mango too?
But suckin mango was de best.

Especially wen yuh tief it from somebody else land.
Remember Spanishman up Malick?
Dey say Spanishman had ah gun but dat didn't stop
we at all.
He had ah wide variety of mango: vere, cora, zabico, starch,
calabash, doo-douce, turpentine, sousay-matin, julie an rose.
Spanishman had mango like peas.
After we full we bag we use tuh siddong by de corner, reach in
de bag, take out de first mango we touch an just start tuh suck.
Wen we empty de bag we use tuh see who could belch de
hardest witout vomitin.
Fuss we belly full.

Yuh remember ah real mango-eating session?
Wen yuh really come out tuh suck mango, yuh doh jus suck one
or two mango an call dat George.
Yuh must suck mango until yuh belly full; until yuh jaws tired;
juice must run down thru yuh fingers an reach yuh elbow an
yuh must lick it orf.
Yuh remember suckin ah mango seed until it white?
Man, it have some seed dat yuh jus have tuh suck an scrape wit
yuh teeth till yuh get out every ounce ah sweetness.
Wen yuh go home yuh have tuh refuse yuh food.
Den yuh mudder go arsk yuh if yuh sick.
"How come yuh pickin yuh food today?
Is all dat mango yuh eatin, nah?
Anyhow, next week is purge fuh everybody."
Yes man, about de Friday before school reopen was senna an
salts fuh everybody.
Dat was tuh clean out yuh system of all de junk yuh eat over de
vacation.
Dat day was steady traffic tuh de latrine.
Boy, de flow was real heavy.
Man use tuh take ah number an stand in line.

Peltin Mango

If yuh couldn't wait, yuh had tuh run by de neighbor quick, quick.
Bad luck fuh you if dem latrine occupied too.
Den yuh had tuh go in de bushes or dig ah hole in de backyard.
Boy, ah tell yuh dem days was someting else.
How yuh could ever forget dem times?

Yuh ever stand up below ah mango tree wen strong breeze blowin?
Mango does fall like rain.
It does have so much mango dat yuh does get bazodee.
Mango hittin yuh in yuh head, yuh back, yuh foot.
All over yuh body.

Yuh ever notice it have some mango tree dat nobody ever use tuh climb.
Was only two ways tuh get dem mangoes.
Wait patiently fuh dem tuh fall: Boop! Booodoop!
Or leggo big stone an big wood in dey tail.
Yes man, peltin mango was plenty fun.
But lookout, oui.
If was ah tree wit spirit, it would pelt back stone an bus yuh head.

Meh pardner, Carlsbury, say he was de best pelter in Mayo Village.
He say he coulda stem ah mango; run below de tree an ketch it before it touch ground; den carry it fuh he gyulfren, Pat.
He was bad fuh days.

Yuh ever listen tuh mango fallin on de galvanize durin de night?
Especially wen rain fallin too.
Man, ah couldn't wait fuh mornin tuh come tuh run out in de yard.
Yuh better wake up early, odderwise yuh fren an dem go pass by an clean up yuh yard fuh yuh.
Me an Sample use tuh go by Pa George before day clean.
Sometimes yuh could bounce up odder fellas dey too.

If yuh see we feelin in de dark fuh mango.
One mornin George pass he han in some dog tutu.
He start tuh cuss; an I start tuh laugh.
Next ting yuh know I put meh bare foot in some.
Both ah we start tuh cuss an laugh.
De dogs take in we tail;
Pa open de back door an start tuh cuss too.
Man, we take orf through de wet bush an scale de fence.
Dat was real fun.
But as ah reach meh back door meh Grandmother greet meh wit de fryin pan.
Wap!
"Yuh say yuh prayers?
If yuh arsk Mr George fuh some mango, ah sure he would give yuh some."
How could I tell she dat de last time we try dat Pa George gi we some soft, squingy, buss-up mango.
Tuh besides dat way didn't have no excitement in it.
So ah take meh two fryin pan tuh head an ah went an say meh prayers.
Someting always in season in Trinidad an Tobago.
If is not Carnival, is Christmas or Easter, or cricket or football.
Havin ah good time always in season in my land.
Even at ah wake fuh de dead, we does celebrate.
Wat! Wit all dat free liquor, food an All Fours, yuh bong tuh have fun.
It hard tuh get bored in Trinidad an Tobago.
Just follow de seasons an yuh life go be happy.

Mama, I'm Confused

"Mama, do you have a minute?"
"Yes, son. What is it?"
"Mama, I'm confused.
How come peace is breaking out all over the world and America is still preparing for war?"
"Because "The Man" says that the best defense is a strong offense.
We have to stay in the forefront of military technology.
Do you understand that?"
"Not really, Mama."
"In addition, they say it is good for our economy."
"Mama, you mean that in order for us to live well,
we have to either make war or prepare for war."
"Seems that way, son. Seems that way.
Boy, how come you're asking all these hard questions?"
"Because I am trying to get answers, Mama,
answers to make sense of my world.
Of our world."

"By the way Mama, what is freedom?
Is freedom in Europe and Asia the same as freedom
in South Africa?
Is there a white freedom and a black freedom?"
How come freedom in Lithuania gets more air time than
freedom for twenty-three million Blacks in South Africa?
Mama, what is freedom?"
"Boy, freedom is the right of choice."
"Choose what, Mama?"
"Mama the T.V. shows that the Russians now have the right to
line up an buy junk food with one week's wage.

Is that right?
Is that a right, Mama?
They now have the right to buy some of the same things that are not good for our health.
Is that freedom?
Mama, are we free?"
"Sometimes I wonder, son. Sometimes I wonder.
Son, why are you suddenly asking me all these difficult questions?"
"Mama, I'm preparing for a debate."
"What's the topic, son?"
"Should America celebrate Black History Month?"
I'm arguing for the continuation of Black History month.
I feel that we need the whole year to really teach and learn our History.
Not "His Story" but "Our Story."
"You're right about that, son. You're right."
"Mama, according to that song, it seems as though the world today is "a ball of confusion".
What can we do, Mama? What can we do?"
"We gots to pray, son.
We just gotta continue praying to the Good Lord."

My Roots

Ah wonder if Miss Maude remember de time she arsk me and George, " Why don't you all go and edify yourselves?"
Was ah Sunday afternoon around two o'clock.
We did come over tuh play wit Carlton an dem.
But as we reach de front steps we see all man had dey book an some ah dem was cryin.
Den Miss Maude spot we an take ah tun in we tail wit she big words an good English.
Boy, we take orf thru de hibiscus fence after makin monkey face behine she back.
Somebody laugh an we hear "Wap".
Shorty shout out; "Oh God Mammy". Miss Maude say, "Shut up, before ah give yuh ah nex one."
We went straight an look up de word,"edify".
We did never hear dat word before.
Thanks Miss Maude, yuh teach we someting dat day.

Is people like Miss Maude an she husband, Mr Alston, dat make Trinidad dear tuh meh.
Anodder unforgettable character from my boyhood days is Pa Elton.
He was ah Blacksmith, ah furrier an ah wheelwright.
Ah used tuh stand fascinated watchin Pa Elton doin he wuk.
Ah used tuh enjoy turnin de furnace tuh make de iron red hot, an den watch him shape it into ah horse shoe.
It was like magic tuh meh eyes.
Pa Elton was he own boss.
An all he chirren, nine ah dem, use tuh help.
How Pa Elton an Mrs Davis raise nine chirren in dem guava days is ah miracle.

Doh tell me it eh have no God.
De odder day ah pass an look fuh Pa Elton.
He cyar see too good now but he recognize meh voice from de first syllable.
He was glad tuh see meh; tuh touch meh; tuh hear meh.
Tears come tuh meh eyes wen ah shake he han; grip still strong from all dat hammerin and hard wuk.
His youngest son, Ranny, is now makin kitchen cabinets in de same workshop. Horse an donkey cart disappearin.
Ranny now is impressin ah new generation.
Ah look around tuh see ah lil boy like me.
Ah see one an ah smile.
Perhaps one day he too go write about Ranny.
Life interestin, oui.

Roots fuh me is walkin in from de Eastern Main Road.
Either dong Third Avenue, Second Avenue or Jogie Road tuh Twelfth Street an notin wat change, remain de same or gone forever.
Is like takin inventory.
My roots spread far an wide in Trinidad and Tobago.
Yes, Tobago too.
My mother, Frances, is from Tobago.
Joe Chapman from Bon Accord was meh grandfather.
Dey use tuh call him Ba Joe.
Dey shudda call him Beau Joe.
He had plenty pickney, so ah have countless uncle an cousin.
Hilda Patrick, who had ah parlor on Milford Road, was meh mudder aunt.
Tanty Hilda was well-known fuh she Bajan.
It was ah heavy sweetbread wit nuff coc'nut.
Ah have roots in Barbados too.
Meh paternal grandmother, Irene Hollingsworth, was from

Bank Hall, St. Michael's.
Ask for Lionel and Keith Foster.

Roots fuh me is characters: like Paray, Bong Tuh Drunk,
Mr. Harewood an hop'n'drop Sonny, de shoemakers.
Mr. Harewood had one greetin: "Say Something."
Sonny never finish yuh job on time.
Ah tink he did like yuh tuh siddong an lime.
Yuh remember Patan?
He was de big, strong Indian man who dey say lift up de heavy roller in Barataria Savannah.
Dey say he strain ah muscle in he leg so he couldn't run fast.
De school chirren use tuh call him names from ah good distance an run.
He was one ah de most feared characters because he coulda pelt big stone good an would even come in school behine yuh.
Even de Headmaster, Rampey, did fraid Patan.

Roots fuh me is places like Sixth Avenue an de Eastern Main Road.
Phantom and Mr. Cummings use tuh sell ice an press on opposite corners.
Mr. Cummings had de best press in de world.
Nowadays dey does call it snowcone.
Before yuh coulda say Jack Robinson, Mr. Cummings woulda shave de ice, press it firmly in ah silver cup, dip it in some red an yellow syrup, collect yuh penny an yuh gorn yuh way suckin.

Sixth Avenue an Fifth Street use tuh be ah train station.
Man use tuh hop orf like starboy in dem Western we use tuh see in Ritz theatre.
Double-ugly in de ticket booth use tuh get vex an call de guard.
Anodder place was de Croisee, de place dat never sleeps,
wey dem badjohns use tuh lime by de icebox.

Up tuh now ah does still get ah powerful feelin wen ah crawl thru de Croisse.

It have some people still fraid de place.

In Aranguez and El Socorro, ah use tuh play it cool.

It had ah time yuh coulda get yuh head bus if yuh walkin too tall down dey.

Dat is one ting with Trinidad, yuh better know wey tuh walk an how tuh walk, otherwise yuh could end up severely hurt or dead.

Yes man, Trinidad an Tobago, an Barbados is people, places, tings and experiences.

Dey in meh blood.

Dats why dey forever in meh thoughts and dreams.

So, accordin tuh Sniper:

'Trinidad is my land and of it I am proud and glad. . .'

We Own Is We Own

Ah gettin mad, mad, mad wit dem so call Yankee from Trinidad.
Yuh go tuh ah basement party pack up wit dem an is only soul, soul, soul.
How de hypocrites so bold?
Dey is more Yankee dan people who born an grow here.
If yuh does see dey face wen we music fill de place.
Dey face does come long, long, like tuh Trinidad dey ain't belong.
Aye, hear nah, yuh know wat ah cyar understand wit dem?
Is wen dey siddong among strangers an dey start talkin bout culture.
First ting dat does come out dey two-tong mout is steelband, calypso and carnival.
Hear dem force-ripe, fresh-water Yankee,
"Man, our Carnival is outa sight.
I tell you Bro, it's really something else.
You should try and dig the scene next year.
Our Carnival is the eighth wonder of the world."
Boy, ah does watch dem an grind meh teeth like ah sugar mill.
But ah waitin patiently fuh dey tail, wen dey invade Piarco again, sportin all dem gaudy threads.
De atmospheere will resound wit WAPS, as I forcefully distribute meh bull tuh dey back.
Hear meh, "Take dis." WAP!
"Wear dese." WAP! WAP!
"Hold dat." Wap!
"Doh ever forget dat..." WAP!
"Yuh own is yuh own."
WAP! WAP!

"To God be the Glory" . . . *Andrae Crouch 1971*

Glossary

Ah .... A, I, of.
Ah mean tuh say... An expression of annoyance, equivalent to, "After all."
All fours....Card game played by four.
All kinda ting....All kinds of things. Everything imaginable.
All man....Everybody.
All yuh.... All of you people. A group.
Ars....As soon as.
Bacalao....Salted cod fish, salt fish.
Bacchanal....Big party. Confusion.
Bad John....A bully. Someone with a violent reputation.
Bad talk....To spread rumors about someone. To illspeak.
Bake....A kind of bread. Dough is fried or roasted.
Bamsee....Rear end. The posterior.
Baron....Timothy Watkins, popular calypsonian.
Bawl like twenty tarzan....To cry excessively.
Bazodee....Giddy or light headed. Confused.
Behin God back....A far off place. Remote part of the country.
Better belly bus' dan good food was'e.... It is better to overeat than to throw away food.
Bhaji.... East Indian for spinach.
Big belly doon-doon....A person with a very large stomach.
Bill Trotman....Popular calypsonian and comedian.
Black cake....Dark colored cake made with fruits soaked in alcohol.
Black puddin....A highly seasoned mixture of animal blood, bread, herbs and spices stuffed into cow's intestines and boiled.
Bokie....A blow to the knuckles, as punishment to the losers in the game of marbles.

Bol' face....Bold face. A pushy person.
Bong Tuh drunk....A person who gets drunk quickly and often.
Boo Booloops....Big and fat and out of shape.
Boo boo man....Bogey man. A fictitious character used to scare children.
Bounce upon....To meet unexpectedly.
Breads....Slang for "brother".
Broko....A person who walks with a limp.
Buh wait nuh....But wait a minute.
Bull boy...A cane or rod-like weapon made from the preserved penis of the cow.
Bump....To swagger with a "hop" and "drop" gait.
Bu'n Bu'n....The burnt portion of any food that sticks to the bottom of the pot.
Buss up shut....Paratha, shredded roti.
By de time....In the meantime.
Callaloo....A thick soup made from dasheen leaves, ochroes, coconut milk, seasoned to taste.
Call dat George....Call it finish. End of the matter.
Calpet....Tap or slap behind the head.
Calypso....A song or musical beat peculiar to Trinidad and Tobago.
Catstraddle....A headlong fall to the ground.
Chalkie....Teacher/Calypsonian, Hollis Liverpool.
Chiney....Chinese.
Chupidness....Stupidness, foolishness.
Cocksure....certain, positive.
Coki-eye....Cock-eyed, cross-eyed.
Crawl....To walk tall and defiant.
Crazy....Edwin Ayoung, popular calypsonian.
Croisse....Pronounced Quaysay. Main junction of the San Juan **area**.
Cut out....To leave suddenly.
Cutlash....Cutlass. Machete.

Cyar....Can't.
Dan....Than.
Dats why....That is why.
De....The.
Deck off....To be well dressed.
Dem....Them.
Den....Then.
Deputy....Mistress, the other woman or man in the menage-a-trois.
Dese....These.
Dey....They.
Dose....Those.
Doo-dup....A two note percussion instrument made from a small round drum beaten with a rubber-tipped stick.
Eat me out....To have visitors 'descend' on your home and eat and drink everything in sight.
Eh....Sometimes used at the end of a plea. Save some fuh me, eh. Used in place of "didn't": He eh come. Used in place of "isn't": Dat eh true.
En'less....Plenty.
Explashiate....To be most vocal in one's comments. To go on and on.
Fatigue....To give someone fatigue. To heckle or tease.
Flannel ball....Lawn tennis ball.
Fo-day mornin....Early dawn.
Fraid....To be afraid; scared.
Fren....Friend.
Fuh....For.
Gazette paper....Newsprint. Old newspapers.
Gi....Give.
Good too bad....Very good. Anything first class.
Guava season....Hard times. Financial strain.
Gyul....Girl, young woman.
Had was tuh....Had to.
Han' swingin....Two long han swingin. Empty-handed.

Without a contribution.

Horn....When the love of your life becomes involved with someone else.

Ice man....Vendor selling ice from a pushcart, truck or stand.

In de bag....It's as good as won. It's all over.

In two twos....Very quickly. A short space of time.

Ironman....Person who 'beats' the iron by striking the brake hub with a short steel rod, with a special rhythm.

Jam....A big, noisy party.

Jokey.... Humorous, funny,

Knocks.... Knuckles.

Leh....Let. Let's.

Leh we....Let us.

Lemme.... Let me, allow me.

Licks....A beating. Physical punishment.

Like peas....Plenty of anything.

Lime....When a small group of people engage in a sometimes pre-arranged activity for pleasure.

Maco....Person who minds other people's business for the purpose of gossip.

Magabones....Very thin person.

Mango chow....Preparation of chopped green mangoes seasoned with pepper and salt.

Mankind....Any number of persons. Also used for "I".

Monkey face....To contort the face in such a way as to stimulate laughter. Also as a rude or insolent gesture.

Nuff....enough, plenty.

Nutten ....Nothing.

Obeah man/woman....Man or woman who practises a kind of witchcraft practised in the West Indies.

Oil dong....Oil down. A food preparation of bread fruit, coconut milk, pigtail, saltmeat, etc.

Ole talk...Idle chatter, social chit-chat.

One set a....A lot of any thing.

Pallet man....A vendor who sells frozen lollies.
Pan....Musical instrument indigenous to Trinidad and Tobago. Tempered oil drums cut to various lengths, grooved sections are tuned to play notes according to scale.
Pan man/woman....One who beats pan or plays the instrument.
Pastelle....Christmas delicacy, made from grated corn stuffed with meat, olives, raisins, etc. wrapped and tied in fig leaves and boiled.
Pee....to urinate.
Pelau.....One pot. Popular quick dish. Cook-up of rice, pigeon peas, chicken, beef and any other ingredients.
Pelt....To throw stones or objects at.
Pessy....A thick reed-like whip used to discipline children at school.
Pickney....A small child.
Pitch oil pan..Vegetable cooking oil tin container. Used for boiling ham, corn, carrying water etc.
Pong....Pound. Gossip or illspeak someone.
Press....Now snowcone. The shaven ice is pressed into a glass before syrup is poured over it.
Punch de creme....Ponchacrema. A potent brew of eggs, milk, rum or brandy, Angostura Bitters and crushed ice. Usually made at Christmas time.
Put away de house....To decorate and spring clean the house.
Rescue....Appointed area of neutrality in kids games of catch, police and thief. Also jail break.
Savannah.....Queen's Park Savannah, a large park, about 232 acres located in the heart of Port of Spain.
Scrunt....Down and out. Penniless.
See-er man....Witch-doctor. One who is supposed to foretell the future by the reading of cards, palms of the hand etc.
Senna....A purgative brewed from the leaves and pods of the senna plant.
Set ah....Lots of.

Shadow....Winston Bailey, popular calypsonian.
Shut....Shirt.
Skater....A home-made scooter.
Smartman....One who tries clever schemes to arrive at a result.
Sniper.... A calypsonian. Composer of "Portrait of Trinidad."
Snowball 'n milk......A mixture of crushed ice, syrup, condensed milk and water.
Slinger Francisco.... The Mighty Sparrow, Calypso King of The World.
Speechify....To talk at length on any subject.
Squingy...Small, dried up. Qualey.
Steelband....Steel Orchestra made up of a series of pans: tenors, seconds, double seconds, guitar, cello, base; iron.
Stick break in yuh ears....Deaf. Harden. Disobedient.
Stick 'em up....Kids game of cowboys and Indians.
Sums....Mathematical problems.
Sunday bes'....Best clothes.
Sunday food......Food considered to be a bit more extravagant than that prepared during the week.
Sweetie....Any confectionery.
Sweet man......A man who is kept by a woman.
Sweet oil....Oil for cooking. Olive oil.
Take uh tun....To set upon.
Tan tan bo hog.... A name applied to any greedy person.
T'ief....A thief. To steal.
Thru....Thru.
Ting....Thing.
Tink....Think.
To besides, an....Besides which. In addition.
Too bad....Very good.
Touto baghai....Everything.
Toute monde....Everybody.
T'ree hole....A game of marbles when three shallow holes are dug and used as part of the game.

Trini....Trinidadian.

True-true....True-blooded.

Twelve t'irty....A movie that starts at 12:30 p.m.

Two-tong....Deceitful.

Upstairs house....A two-story dwelling.

Vere....One of the better-known varieties of mango.

Village ram....A womanizer, especially in a small village.

Vup.... In cricket, to swing the bat as hard as possible.

Water on duck back.... Futile, a waste of time

Way yuh talkin!....A boastful expression. Also of admiration or agreement. Superlative- beyond words.

Whe-whe....An illegal game based on impulse, dreams and other portents where numbers correspond with 'marks'. Anyone who has the correct number or symbol is a winner.

Win' ball cricket.... Cricket played with a lawn tennis ball instead of the traditional leather ball.

Wit....With.

Witout....Without.

Woulda....Would have.

Wuk....Work.

Yuh tink it easy?....It is not as easy as you think. Also believe it or not.

Zabico....A variety of mango.

Zwill....A thin person.